DIRTY BUSIN

OR... THE STRATEGIC IMPLICATIONS OF CRIMINALITY, UNETHICAL CONDUCT AND BLACK ECONOMIC PRACTICE ON LEGITIMATE BUSINESS

DR PETER J. HURLEY

Dedication

To Bayan, Joe and Ted, three of the most lovable but disreputable rascals ever to walk the earth, and a few other despicable miscreants from whom I learned much about the darker and undesirable side of the commercial world, even though I'd wished I'd avoided learning the hard way.

Also, to all those who wish to steer a straighter business course while avoiding being screwed over by those of a less noble disposition, and most of all, to my parents and family who gave me a value set, strength of character and support to carry on.

"Experience is the hardest kind of teacher.

It gives you the test first and the lesson afterward."

Oscar Wilde

* * *

Preface

Despite the huge body of literature on business administration, business law and risk management, and even with the growing awareness of the implications of unethical corporate conduct, *Dirty Business* is still largely a taboo subject only whispered about behind closed doors. After all, when one suspects someone in an organisation is taking a bung or defrauding a company, it's not exactly a topic that's commercially prudent or safe to discuss openly. Yet it's exactly what professionals and senior managers should be able to identify and ideally have the knowledge to prevent. But having high intelligence and a good business or legal education or even being an attorney at law is no safeguard against being ripped off by the unethical and criminally minded players in the real world of 21st-century business.

Much can be gained from understanding business law, but in the opinion of this author, lawyers seldom make for good commercially minded businessmen. Businessmen, meanwhile, frequently lack the legal expertise and commercial experience they need to avoid trouble. To square this circle, this book has been written from the perspective of an experienced business practitioner, *not a lawyer or academic*, for fellow would-be business practitioners. It's not a compendium of 'tricks and strategies' to misguide, deceive or do down others. This work is intended to be a broad methodological review of 'what and why' things can go wrong in business and commerce when encountering dishonourable individuals and corporations. In reality, this book is the tugging open of a curtain which has cloaked a largely clandestine subject, but hopefully through the shedding of light, this work will illuminate ways to avoid some of the business world's snake pits, bear traps and mine fields.

* * *

Contents

Figures

1. Introduction

I was midway through a technical career as an industrial chemist and mulling over the drab prospect of being a wage slave until I picked up my old age pension when I came to the realisation shared by many: self-employment in some project – any project – would be more fulfilling. I well recall talking with my mother during one of our many conversations around the kitchen table while she was baking, telling her that I was going to undertake an MBA, and pursue a commercial career, with the long-term aim of working for myself at some point. My mother, the most intelligent and thoughtful woman I've ever met, was usually highly supportive in whatever endeavours I or my siblings ever pursued and usually, even where she had reservations, would hold back and let us know that whatever happened we had her love and support. However, on this occasion I could see real concern in her eyes. *"Are you sure?"* she said, and, shaking her head, added, *"We're not business people"*. I thought perhaps that her concerns were in large part due to her father's experience. Though an engineer by trade, he used to own a small grocery store in Barrow-in-Furness back in the 1920s. He did well up until the commencement of the Great Depression in 1930, whereupon, like so many others, he went bust. Much to my grandmother's annoyance, the root of the problem was that he gave too much credit to those who he probably knew could not pay. The simple truth was in those dark times he didn't have it in him to refuse food to those who might otherwise literally starve. My mother had witnessed much of the misery of that time, both through the struggles of her parents and at a young age having worked as a manageress of a pawnbrokers in Lancaster in the early to mid-1930s.

On reflection, I realised that the root of my mother's concern was that she believed to succeed in business you needed to be emotionally 'hard' and potentially 'cut throat' in your outlook, and we had been brought up with what may be termed low church Christian ethics, which in her eyes were essential traits for a 'right-minded' person, yet would be undesirable, indeed a debilitating career factor, for a 'businessman'. With my mother's words in mind, I duly embarked on my MBA at Manchester Business School and a subsequent career at the sharp end of commercial management in the chemical sector. I can honestly say that I have never been party to any crime of moral turpitude or commercial dishonesty and have always backed away from any type of unethical conduct. I don't profess to be a saint. I'm just a guy who's had to put up with a lot! Yet my career hasn't been without success. While I haven't risen to great heights in the boardroom of any multinational, I have started several highly profitable multi-million-pound-turnover businesses from scratch. So, despite my mother's misgivings, it is perfectly possible to be both commercially successful and conduct business with good ethics.

Today we view 'ethics' in business as an essential part of good corporate governance. Moreover, it's not just about abiding by the laws of the land but 'doing the right thing' in the eyes of the public and critically those you would seek to positively influence, such as customers, the wider market, prospective employees and industry regulators. Business textbooks and the papers are littered with examples of reputational damage done by the lack of strategic attention paid to ethics by corporations and high net worth individuals in conducting their business activities. However, it is a cold hard fact of life that if dubious business practices and outright criminal conduct didn't pay, commercial crime would not exist, and incidents of reputational damage would not occur. The ugly truth of the matter is that they do. Unethical conduct that borders on illegality is commonplace, and in some global markets it is almost the business cultural norm. Despite my measured success with ethical conduct in business, and having had the full benefit of a high quality formal business education, my path would have been a lot smoother had I been educated in the harsh realities of some of the unethical practices I had encountered or witnessed en route.

For the purposes of those who wish to follow an ethical path in business, and hoping that they avoid much of the pain and tribulations that I encountered during my career, I have written this text on what is to many a somewhat taboo subject of the strategic implications of criminality, unethical conduct and black economic practice on legitimate business, or put simply *'Dirty Business'*. It is by no means an exhaustive study on the subject, but it is intended to give a flavour of what does happen in the 'real world' of business. So, in the words of one somewhat cynical old man wizened by adversity, yes, you can conduct business ethically and be successful, but you can do the same with a lot less pain if you're just a little 'streetwise' and take care because there are less scrupulous individuals and corporations who have opted to play by different rules.

* * *

2. The Symptoms of an Unethical Organisation

To most, the negative consequences of unethical or criminal conduct are simply being found out and being embarrassed, having to pay the fine or at worst have a few fall guys do time. But it's not that simple. Where you have an enterprise, be it a corporate entity or individual that has chosen to occupy the grey area between what is legal and ethical as deemed by the majority's moral standards, and what is expedient but unethical or criminal, then that entity is but for one false move at risk of destroying its hard-won reputation overnight. That false move being an event that brings the glaring light of the entity's unethical conduct or criminal wrongdoing into the view of regulators, the market in which the company operates or the wider public.

Within business studies literature, unethical conduct has been likened to a corporate sickness. Cialdini et al[1] in their article "The Hidden Costs of Organisational Dishonesty", propose that an organisation that regularly teaches, encourages, condones or allows the use of dishonest tactics in external dealings will suffer from three malignancies, which they categorise by the processes involved. I broadly illustrate these below and would propose to extend their approach and add a fourth to their original list:

(1) **Reputational Degradation**: The consequence of a systematically dishonest organisation is that it will inevitably develop a poor reputation. To those outside the company (customers, suppliers, partner organisations, regulators, or the media and through them the general public), reputation matters. A US poll of the general population in 2003 found that 80% of the public would consider ethical reputation would have an impact on their decision whether to buy goods or services from that organisation.[2] Thus, the unethical organisation might find its sales deteriorating with repeat business becoming less

prevalent. In the same poll, when questioned, 75% asserted that the honesty of a corporation's behaviour would influence their decision to buy stock in that company. If ethical standing influences investment decisions, it can be realistically conjectured that it will also influence other financial stakeholders in the company, such as banks and other lending institutions. Poor ethics implies increased fiscal risk. To lenders, that translates into reducing lines of credit to the organisation, and likely to increasing onerous terms, which in turn may spell doom for the organisation. Ultimately this manifests itself as a slide in the value of shareholder capital.

(2) **(Mis)matches between Values of Employees and the Organisation**: Where the organisation is dishonest in the eyes of its workforce an ethical gap develops. Workers perceive this as an effective breach in the psychological contract between themselves and the organisation, which in turn leads to loss of loyalty. It can manifest itself as lower job satisfaction, lower productivity, increased sickness and absenteeism, and increased staff turnover, with the most highly skilled workers, i.e. those most able to redeploy, being lost first. In contrast, potentially dishonest employees who share the values of the organisation will be attracted to it. When this occurs, we can imagine that the organisation becomes caught in an ethical death spiral, leading to lower productivity, higher costs and potentially to the organisation's demise.

(3) **Increased Surveillance**: The diminished relationship and implied lack of trust arising from the above malignancies between workers and corporation manifests itself in dysfunctional behaviour and low productivity. It also leads to increased genuine sickness through worker stress and related conditions such as anxiety and depression, thereby compounding

absenteeism problems. To counter these issues, a typical organisational response is to increase employee surveillance with tighter, more intrusive oversight of work and increased regulation of internal conduct. This leads to an oppressive workplace culture which can further exacerbate deteriorating industrial relations. Ultimately, excessive monitoring becomes self-defeating.

(4) Cause Harm to Persons within and without the Bounds of the Organisation: Unethical organisations hurt people. If a company is run such that it's screwing its external stakeholders, suppliers and customers, it's hardly the type of organisation that at the same time will be paying full heed to health, safety and environmental legislation, or employee rights in its own operations. It will also be unlikely that it is carrying out the essentials of commercial good governance, e.g. not holding regular stockholder meetings and being less than transparent in its financial dealings, other than meeting the absolute minimum reporting requirements. Plus, it's equally unlikely that it will adhere to industry standards and legislative requirements relating to the sale of its goods or services. When organisations or their products harm people, it usually comes to the attention of regulators and sometimes the media, perhaps not as one big issue, but as a trickle of lesser events.

As the malignancies illustrate, for both corporates and individuals, in business there are real long-term consequences to loss of reputation. These symptoms ultimately manifest themselves in long-term detrimental harm to shareholder value. Reputation can take years to build but can be lost in an apparent moment of rashness. The reality will more likely be that the moment of rashness was just the tip of the iceberg, and prior there were many such rash incidents which never made it to the regulator's attention or into the public domain. Rebuilding a lost reputation takes even longer than to originally earn. It's not simply an issue of paying the fine and overcoming a little embarrassment.

In outlining the malignant traits of the unethical organisation, and its associated risk of doing business with the same, the business practitioner needs to be aware not just who he's doing business with but what are their ethics. To this end, I've always found the 'Duck' principle invaluable. If it walks like a duck and quacks like a duck, it's a duck. In assessing potential customers, suppliers and business partners, the spectrum of malignancies provides us with a working template by which we can detect the probability of whether we are dealing with an ethical corporation or not. Once identified, then at least, the practitioner will have the informed option to deal at arm's length, walk or run away.

How does a corporation become unethical? A company is a business machine in the same way as a computer. Its inputs are capital and raw materials and its outputs are its goods and services and value for its stakeholders. Its hardware is the material and human assets of the firm. Its software is the data and business decisions made by its management, with each individual decision being an effective 'condition statement sequence' in its program. Though frequently hard to trace, the root cause for an organisation to become corrupt of purpose and develop malignancies can require as little as one malfunctioning key component, i.e. an 'individual manager' causing or influencing faulty 'managerial decision-making'. Take a CEO with a tendency to make unethical judgment calls, given enough time, and a failure to correct their deficiencies, a whole organisation can be subverted to the point where its commercial viability is threatened.

3. The Drivers of Individual and Organisational Unethical Conduct

For conscious unethical conduct, be it organisational or individual, there are three prerequisites: motive, means and opportunity. In considering motivational factors, these are the drivers that lead the ethically corrupt to seek means and opportunity by which their unethical intent can be realised.

Most people believe that poverty, family background, low self-esteem, alcohol and drug abuse are factors which explain why some people commit crimes or engage in unethical conduct – but they don't tell the full story. In a commercial environment, I would personally discount poverty as an overriding factor, since the perpetrators of 'white-collar crime' are employed and usually only have the opportunity to enact or control such events if they are in a reasonably well-paid senior position.

Following the spectacular large-scale economy shaking corporate frauds at WorldCom and Enron in the US, Bucy et al[3] conducted a wide-ranging survey of legal professionals with extensive experience engaged in the prosecution and defence of white-collar criminals. Their findings open with the bluntly stated observation:

> "Why do talented, bright, highly educated, successful people, who have 'made it', risk it all by lying, stealing, and cheating, especially when what they're stealing is not much compared to what they have? The simple answer is, 'because they can'."

This brings home the stark reality that opportunity or rather the lack of oversight that permits the opportunity to be taken relatively risk free is itself the oxygen on which the flames of unethical conduct and criminality feed. Given opportunity, not all people succumb to temptation so what is it about some individuals and corporations that leads them to become thieves?

The Bucy et al study drew the conclusions that white-collar crime was on the increase and more especially so where the 'criminal' was actually a whole corporation. They identified that, within the ethically dysfunctional corporation, the dysfunctional behaviour was not simply about flaws in the character of individuals but a condition of corporate culture that created 'situations' and 'social bonds', that would give rise to an environment that encouraged white-collar crime. In particular, salary incentives wherein there was an excessive focus on profits served as inducement to fraud, and this was exacerbated where the organisation omitted key elements of compliance and ethics.

Bucy et al concluded that within groups of white-collar criminals operating in unethical corporations there was a hierarchy of participants, which they broadly categorised as 'leaders' and 'followers'. The bulk of white-collar criminals could be classified as followers. Followers by nature were placid, nonaggressive individuals who facilitate but don't instigate unethical behaviour. Such individuals were more easily deterred by good corporate governance and oversight where internal and external audit existed with adequate systems to monitor compliance. However, leaders were a different matter. Bucy et al describe them as being typical 'Type A' personalities: intelligent, cunning, successful, prone to risk taking, aggressive, narcissistic and charismatic. Whilst white-collar criminals were found to be predominantly male, 'leaders' tended to be 'upper middle class' and 'well-educated'. They were primarily motivated by greed and beyond greed, by a sense of entitlement, arrogance and competitiveness. As additional motivating factors, some participants identified fear of failure or loss of status, lifestyle or job, while others were responding to pressure to meet financial goals. Interestingly, less than 5% of the participants expressed the view that white-collar criminals were amoral or evil. This in part could be down to cultural issues, as today we still largely view 'white-collar crime' as a 'victimless crime' and its perpetrators as more Robin Hood than Sheriff of Nottingham. Beyond motivation, Bucy et al identified eight personality

9

characteristics within leaders that were deemed to fuel white-collar crime:

(1) Need for control.

(2) Bullying.

(3) Charisma, empowering leader to instigate and manipulate.

(4) Fear of failing motivated by fear of loss of professional and financial standing.

(5) Greed, both individual and corporate.

(6) Narcissism.

(7) Lack of integrity.

(8) Lack of social conscience.

Decision-making is the core element of the software of business. Individuals making business choices can sometimes be faced with ethical dilemmas and choices to be made. An individual can sometimes make a mistake, but in intrinsically unethical individuals, those mistakes exhibit a consistent long-term pattern of behaviour. When such a person is placed in a leadership role within an organisation they may well influence the decision-making processes of others to create a corporate culture that biases decision-making toward unethical outcomes. Do all individuals in corporations making such decisions ultimately have character flaws leading them to make irrational and unethical errors of judgment?

3.1 Rational Business Decision-Making and Its Subversion

Arriving at a business decision or even negotiating a business transaction is no more, no less than dealing with an exchange of information, evaluating it and, if to be successful, creating a meeting of minds, ideally in a rational and constructive manner, to meet a mutually beneficial outcome. Yet, in the real world, things don't always work out this way. Consider the academic exercise called 'The Prisoner's Dilemma', which is an example in game theory that shows why two completely 'rational' individuals might not cooperate, even if it appears that it is in their best interests to do so. It was originally framed by Merrill Flood and Melvin Dresher working for the RAND Corporation in 1950.

The game, as originally conceived, pictures two criminals who are arrested and imprisoned. Each prisoner is in solitary confinement with no means of communicating with the other. The prosecutors lack sufficient evidence to convict the pair on the principal charge. They hope to get both sentenced to a year in prison on a lesser charge. Simultaneously, the prosecutors offer each prisoner a bargain. Each prisoner is given the opportunity either to betray the other by testifying that the other committed the crime or to cooperate with the other by remaining silent. The offer is:

- If A and B each betray the other, each of them serves two years in prison.

- If A betrays B but B remains silent, A will be set free and B will serve three years in prison (and vice versa).

- If both remain silent, each will only serve one year in prison (on the lesser charge).

It is implied that the prisoners will have no opportunity to reward or punish their partner other than the prison sentences they get, and that their decision will not affect their reputation in the future. Thus, decision-making must rely largely on the prisoner's external motivators. Given the simplest interpretation of the game and the equal odds of outcome for both parties, the presumed lack of concern for their fellow criminal's plight and the equal probability of all choices, if A betrays B (or vice versa), he will at worst serve two years and has an equal chance of going free. Whereas to stay silent, A will at worst serve three years and at best one year. Because betraying a partner offers a greater reward than cooperating with him, all purely rational self-interested prisoners would betray the other, and so though an apparently dysfunctional outcome results to the mutual detriment of the parties, the only possible logical outcome for two purely rational prisoners is for them to betray each other.

The interesting part of this result is that pursuing individual reward logically leads both of the prisoners to betray, when they would get a better reward if they both kept silent. In reality, humans display a systemic bias towards cooperative behaviour in this and similar games, much more so than predicted by simple models of 'rational' self-interested action. This can be attributed to the contribution to decision-making from the individual's internal value set.

The prisoner's dilemma teaches us several things. The outcome of the game in the given example favours mutual betrayal based on rational self-interest, given the rules of the game and the balance of rewards or punishments for the decision-making options. Different and perhaps a less clear outcome may be forecast if, for instance, the punishment for the more serious charge was death. This would imply that the surviving individual would live with the residual guilt of having caused another's demise. Alternatively, if both criminals were longstanding members of the same gang where there were bonds of loyalty this would also conflict with and potentially override self-interest. The variations in outcome teach us that people make choices and as a consequence behave as a function of their individual reward and punishment systems in addition to their internal rule systems or character. Furthermore, apparent unethical organisational behaviour may not be down to individual bad ethics or ill intent but to the dysfunctional design of the corporate reward and punishment systems. For example, where a corporation financially rewards individuals, departments or subsidiaries and focuses only on that year's results, and demotes or punishes those not making targets, individuals can collectively be motivated to take unethical decisions to preserve wealth, reputation and personal or institutional power. Such action promulgates an organisation focusing on tactics and driven by short-term expediency, potentially at the expense of the strategic needs and long-term viability of the business.

Speaking hypothetically, I wonder whether this was what motivated the whizz kid who first came up with the bright idea for affixing payment protection insurance (PPI) to financial service products without disclosing the same to vendors, and how long did that individual stay with the firm after receiving that first massive bonus? Does that person feel concern for the fines placed on his old firm and guilt every time they see a PPI claim firm's advertisement on the TV or gets an unsolicited call from a call centre pushing the same?

If we can modify the game's rules, rewards or punishments such that the rational outcome can be changed, then logically, we can apply this principle in the real world when we engage in organisational design of remuneration systems, business dealings, negotiation and contract with other parties. We could then redirect the available options and potential rewards or negative consequences, making clear what the rational logical conclusion is to meet the desired and sustained functionality, meeting of minds and cooperation. A primary consideration of negotiation and contract has to be not to get trapped in the prisoner's dilemma, where the logical rational outcome for the available options will be that the other party behaves dysfunctionally or worse still – shafts you.

3.2 Irrational Decision-Making

The prisoner's dilemma teaches us that the forecast outcome is an application of logic and that the players will act in rational self-interest. I came into business from a highly logical scientific world but the commercial side of business sometimes isn't like that. In business, there is a higher probability of encountering psychopathic behaviour. You don't normally get psychopaths in a technical laboratory environment, that is, unless you've stitched them together yourself from salvaged body parts of uncertain provenance and thrown in a high voltage blast of electricity for good measure! Psychopaths make up about 1% of the general population and as much as 25% of male offenders in US Federal correctional facilities.[4] Psychopathic personalities exhibit egocentricity, selfishness, self-aggrandising behaviour and a lack in empathy and conscience. They are not team players as they generally are too selfish and have difficulties in managing and keeping effective teams together. They tend not to take personal responsibility for their mistakes, but their lack of conscience and selfishness would not inhibit them from taking credit for the achievements of others. Whilst they may perform effectively and maintain control under the eye of superiors, they can tend to express uncontrolled emotional behaviour when out of view, which can make them great at managing up – but difficult to work with and for. Understandably, they are frequently socially dysfunctional. Notwithstanding the aforementioned, psychopaths with traits of ruthlessness, selfishness, narcissism and self-promotion can be highly successful in commercial and corporate environments. Additionally, psychopaths may be charismatic, charming and adept at manipulating one-on-one interactions. Charismatic people are not necessarily psychopaths[5] but there is a high degree of correlation between charismatic leadership and psychopathic behavioural traits.[6]

Psychopaths generally have all the necessary skills required for a career in politics or the boardroom. According to Dutton,[7] the top four careers for psychopaths are CEOs, lawyers, TV and radio media personalities and salespeople. According to Pearlman[8] in one Australian study as many as 21% of senior executives studied were psychopaths. Psychopaths are understandably more common at higher levels in corporate organisations where their style can cause a ripple effect throughout an organisation, setting the tone for an entire corporate culture with a detrimental impact on corporate ethics.[9] Whilst psychopaths are more common in business and leadership positions, is it fair to judge all those with psychopathic traits as potentially unethical or criminal? Mahmut et al[10] in their study "The characteristics of non-criminals with high psychopathy traits: Are they similar to criminal psychopaths", disclose that there is a spectrum of psychopathic behaviour between those with low and high psychopathic traits which they denote as High-P and Low-P. They deduce while both criminal and non-criminal High-P psychopaths exhibit low empathy indicative of orbital frontal cortex dysfunction, the criminal group exhibited more extreme traits associated with interpersonal-affective and antisocial features of psychopathic behaviour and that these features were independent of IQ. However, that doesn't mean all High-P psychopaths that should be behind bars are, but it implies a correlation between High-P psychopathic traits and criminal and unethical conduct. The cynical might say the only difference between a criminal and non-criminal High-P psychopath is an indictment and conviction.

From the above, you might well reason that you will likely come across or have already met psychopaths as colleagues, clients or even business competitors. Though I'm not clinically qualified to make a diagnosis, I believe I have worked for at least three in my career and have come across many others. I wouldn't go as far as Pearlman in ascribing psychopathic behaviour to one in five senior executives but I'd say he was close, with some specific industries fostering more than others.

Though it might be said that psychopaths, being free from emotional sensitivities, are thereby more likely to look at issues with a cold hard rational eye, the implications are, when in business dealings or negotiating with them, they may not be as interested in seeking a fair win-win outcome. They may be more interested in personal reward and how it makes them look rather than the deal meeting the needs of the organisation. Acting *rationally* by its definition implies the conformity of one's beliefs with one's reasons to believe, or of one's actions with one's reasons for action. If the decision maker's beliefs and value set and internal rules structure are divergent from those of the corporation or wider society, then clearly what may be rational to the psychopathic decision maker could be perceived as irrational to others. Psychopaths may be of high IQ but they are debilitated in one key area, human interaction, with a tendency to selfishness and lack of capacity to empathise with others. These traits can be key blocks to effective interpersonal communication. Consider this: how can you effectively manage the key assets of a business – its people or management team – if you have such a communication problem? Given their traits, psychopaths would likely be less cognisant of ethical issues such as the health and safety of their subordinates and their legal obligations of a fiduciary duty of care to them and the wider public. The implications are in business that High-P individuals are more likely to take decisions through what Eugene Soltes termed *'flawed intuition'*, in his book *'Why They do it – Inside the Mind of the White-Collar Criminal'*.[11] Such decisions, although rational in their minds, are at odds with the declared objectives and long-term well-being of their company and the values of an ethical corporation and wider society and thus are perceptibly irrational to others.

3.3 The Ability to Differentiate between a Real Leader and a 'Leader'

There are varied approaches, or 'styles' of leadership and management. Based on different assumptions and theories, the style an individual uses in any given circumstance will encompass a combination of their beliefs, values, preferences and experiences, as well as the organisation's culture and norms, which will encourage some styles of leadership and discourage others. Managerial styles can even vary at differing levels in the same organisation. Without limitation, the differing defined positive management styles are described as Charismatic, Perceptive, Situational, Transactional, Transformational, Quiet, Servant, plus others too numerous to mention. Each has its own merits and demerits in differing circumstances.

For at least the last 30 years, charismatic leadership as a style has been much favoured, especially by backers of corporate finance and human resource professionals filling high-profile roles. Max Weber in 1947 first described the concept of charismatic leadership as stemming from subordinates' (or 'followers') perceptions that the leader is endowed with exceptional skills or talents. There are many descriptions of the qualities that characterise what is broadly defined as 'charismatic leadership'. However, the core element of what is deemed charismatic leadership is being a good communicator, being persuasive and motivating by emotion and inspiration rather than dictât in the manner of an autocratic leader. Charismatic leadership is viewed as almost the antithesis of transactional leadership, which focuses on increasing efficiency through established systems and procedures and is more concerned with following existing rules rather than making organisational change. Transactional leadership tends to be found in organisations that have evolved beyond the chaotic 'no-rules' stage of a start-up entrepreneurial development into the duller and mundane type of organisation that Mintzberg[12] described as a 'machine bureaucracy'. Thus, charismatic leadership qualities, when combined with the confidence and self-belief to challenge the status quo, are a very powerful blend, deemed essential for senior executives in large corporations seeking to be fast growing and entrepreneurial in approach. Similarly, these qualities are thought ideal for leaders to be capable of shaking up and revitalising machine bureaucracies. Therefore, almost to the detriment of other styles, 'charismatic leadership' has been most attractive to human resources professionals and board members alike when filling those crucial top slots in corporations. However, in a world post Worldcom, Enron and the 2008 Banking Crisis, many have questioned the HR and top company boardroom fascination with 'Charisma'. For example, from their studies Stadler and Dyer[13] have drawn the conclusion that when it comes to sustainable performance a charismatic leadership style can be detrimental to an organisation's sustainability, stating:

> *"In a study of 100-year-old European corporations, we found that leaders of the higher-performing companies were often not charismatic – and were, in fact,* less *likely to be charismatic than the leaders of the lower-performing companies. The problem with charismatic leaders is that exceptional powers of persuasion make it easy for them to overcome resistance and opposition to their chosen course of action. If your company is heading in the right direction, a charismatic leader will get you there faster. Unfortunately, if you're heading in the wrong direction, charisma will also get you there faster."*

What is really required in the start-up, high-growth and turnaround situation is a 'transformational leader', who by the very definition has what it takes to bring about change. Transformational leaders are also charismatic, but they are also noted for leading high performing groups and teams, and developing followers' leadership capacity, as much as helping the group or organisation to change and innovate.

There is frequently confusion in assessing the difference between a charismatic leadership style of the 'transformational leader' and the 'charisma' displayed by intelligent High-P individuals. They can have similar traits outside their obvious charisma, being unconventional in outlook and behaviour, and personal risk takers. Where they differ is in their ability to work with and through others, and their ability to view situations encompassing empathy with others. In some texts, psychopaths are declared unable to form and hold teams together. The reality is not so cut and dried. In situations where the team is effectively pre-existing or formed by convention, such as a company's board, one should not underestimate the capacity of team members to self-organise and work around a problematic team leader. Both High-P individuals and transformational leaders can form teams and give clear direction. However, the High-P led team will have a tendency to long-term dysfunctionality owing to their leader's psychopathic trait of lack of empathy and intolerance of any perceived challenge to their leadership. The High-P individual is not perceptive to the wants and needs of team members so usually fails to move in a timely manner to head-off or resolve interpersonal conflicts. They are particularly prone to lack of remorse and unwilling to take responsibility for their errors, but they are happy to take the credit for others' efforts. Thus, a High-P individual will take personal credit for the team and give none individually to his subordinates. Whereas the transformational leader, in his capacity as a mentor will give credit where it's due and reward individuals for their achievements. The High-P individual's self-belief may be so high, they can believe that they are infallible, and hence lead their followers like lemmings over the abyss, even when they have received adequate warning from others. A High-P individual will be prone to narcissism. Their self-absorption or need for admiration and worship can lead to their followers questioning their leadership. Critically, they are usually intolerant of individuals whom they view as challengers to their authority or irreplaceability. Thus, a High-P executive will usually have no successors within their scope of influence when they come to leave their position, thereby complicating succession planning. In contrast, the transformational leader will be a teacher and mentor, grooming his replacement. Having higher capacity to empathise with others, the transformational leader will have cognisance of his fiduciary duty to his staff and will endeavour to keep them from harm's way. He will also likely have a commitment to wider professional ethical standards of behaviour. In flat teams lacking a hierarchy and self-organising, as in the case of a typical Agile project group, leadership will naturally gravitate to the centre of expertise within the group. As the project proceeds and different types of expertise are employed, the leadership will naturally migrate within the team as the project evolves to require differing technical or functional leadership, perhaps passing through the hands of several persons over the progression of the project. Transformational managers would be comfortable in such environments, but the same would be an anathema to the High-P charismatic leader and bringing them into conflict with the natural migration of leadership within the team.

3.4 Macro Economic Factors that Impact Culture and Decision-Making

There is a widely held belief that certain national and regional cultures are more conducive to unethical and criminal conduct. Such beliefs are supported by publications such as the "Corruption Perceptions Index" (CPI).[14] Transparency International (TI)[15] (TI) has published the CPI since 1995, annually ranking countries *"by their perceived levels of corruption, as determined by expert assessments and opinion surveys."* The CPI generally defines corruption as "the misuse of public power for private benefit". TI is a lobby organisation based in Brussels that seeks to influence EU regulators and is associated with the Transparency International Secretariat (TI-S) based in Berlin. A brief study of the CPI 2015 serves to reinforce perceived stereotypes of the developed West, i.e. European and North American countries being bastions of good business practice and ethical conduct, with Scandinavian countries taking four of the top six places, with Switzerland, Germany, United Kingdom and United States, all being highly ranked 7th, 10th, equal 10th and 16th respectively out of 167 countries in total. Less well-developed banana republics, dictatorships, former communist states and countries in the throes of war or insurgency duly rank in the Index's lower reaches.

Whilst developed countries are clearly wealthy, have a well-established civil society, comparatively good governance and rule of law, the CPI can give a misleading impression of the developed West being clean, uncorrupted and having a benign business environment. Before smug Westerners sit down with their mug of cocoa in hand to watch the 10 o'clock news reporting on the wars and disorder in all the basket case nations of the world, they would do well to reflect that it's a sad feature that the pain of the developing world is in good measure the fault of the developed Western nations, as they provide a stable and attractive investment environment for corrupt elites from developing countries to launder and stash away their ill-gotten gains.

As such, the Western investment system actually acts as a stimulus for corruption and criminality in developing nations. This attraction has been enhanced by certain Western nations who have shrouded such dealings by opaque financial reporting regulations, lax tax regimes, numbered bank accounts and banking secrecy laws. In addition, they have also made it possible to hide beneficial ownership of assets and corporations behind nominee directors, directors who are not 'real' persons, trust funds, and all supported by an array of tax haven countries dotted around the world who are intimately integrated into the West's major financial centres. Public assets illegally obtained from developing countries are often hidden in banks located in the financial centres of developed countries. Global Financial Integrity estimates the losses from developing countries were between US$723 billion and US$844 billion per year in 2009.[16] In global economic terms it's only 0.01% of GDP, but still way above the individual GDP of all but the world's top 16 economies. Given the huge sums of money involved and our insight into human nature and the psyche of the businessman, it is understandable that within the West's banking hubs of New York, London, Frankfurt and Zurich there will inevitably be unethical and criminal individuals and corporations prepared to look the other way. Considering the scale of such black economic practice and the numbers of people involved, many of whom by necessity must be professionals – bankers, accountants and lawyers needed to support such activity – it is inconceivable that the sum of their individual behaviours will not adversely impact the professional culture within the West's finance centres. The culture of the finance industry by its very nature impacts on all commerce. Therefore, it would be unreasonable to assume that its culture would not impact on wider business. Indeed, it would be hypocritical to say that Western businesses and its businessmen were far better behaved than their third-world equivalents. Consider France with its moderate ranking of 23rd in the CPI. Yet in November 2015, the French power and transportation company, Alstom S.A., pleaded guilty in the US Federal Court to charges under the US Foreign Corrupt

Practices Act (US-FCPA), and was fined US$772 million in connection with a widespread corruption scheme involving tens of millions of dollars in secret bribes paid to government officials in countries around the world, including Indonesia, Saudi Arabia and Egypt.[17] Sweden is 3rd in the CPI 2015, yet the Swedish-Finnish firm TeliaSonera that is 37% owned by the Swedish state was hit with a record fine of US$1.4 billion under the US-FCPA, for paying millions of dollars in bribes to secure business in Uzbekistan,[18] which comes in at 153rd in the index. The previous record fine holder was Siemens of Germany (10th in the CPI 2015) who were hit with a US$800 million fine in 2008.[19] Switzerland 7th in the CPI is the home of FIFA and Sepp Blatter, whose long-running antics include allegations of breaching general rules of conduct and ethics, disloyalty, allowing conflicts of interest, improperly offering and accepting gifts and other benefits, and bribery and corruption.[20] These will have undoubtedly tarnished both the reputation of the Football Association and further tarnished the reputation of Switzerland, a country long famed for its banking secrecy laws, making it friendly towards tax evaders and illicit deal makers. It is evident that there is a problem with the CPI as a measure of corruption, primarily due to its definition of corruption as *"the misuse of public power for private benefit"*, thereby omitting the impact of inter-business corruption. I suspect that reality is that the apparent ignoring of the latter is down to the fact that though it undoubtedly exists, it is by its clandestine nature almost impossible to measure. Until, that is, it surfaces as a US-FCPA indictment.

The Organisation for Economic Co-operation and Development (OECD) Anti-Bribery Convention, adopted in 1997, requires each signatory country to make foreign bribery a crime for which individuals and enterprises can be held responsible. Prior to that, offering bribes to foreign public officials to obtain contracts were a widespread way of doing business in many OECD countries,[21] excepting the United States, Canada, United Kingdom and Poland, where the offer, agreement to pay, soliciting, acceptance or the payment itself was and remains a criminal offence. Bribery has been compounded by several governments that acted in complicity by offering favourable tax treatment for bribery payments, which could be written off as expenses. Notable amongst them were Switzerland and core EU countries: Germany, Austria, Netherlands, Belgium, France Luxembourg and Portugal. In other jurisdictions, bribes were classified as 'entertainment expenses' and deemed not to be a deductible expense against tax. German-speaking Europe is a particular problem.[22] Prior to 2000 when it became illegal to bribe public officials in Germany, Bloomberg News reported that cartel-like pricing added 20% to 30% to the cost of public contracts.[23] But despite Germany being a signatory to the OECD convention, in 2007 it was alleged in the Siemens case that the company had created €400 million in slush funds, for bribes aimed at securing lucrative contracts abroad. Switzerland, another OECD convention signatory, implemented bribery laws to criminalise bribes to foreign public officials in the early 2000s. Yet, obscenely, even into 2016, bribes to non-government persons and fines were still tax-deductible expenses, with the Swiss government not due to debate proposed changes in tax legislation until December 2016.[24]

Western governments, rightly and sometimes wrongly, pillory newly emerging and developing nations such as Russia, China, India and Brazil for their weak democratic practices and ethical conduct, or in some cases the lack of them. To be fair, these nations don't have long traditions as stable democracies, whereas the West does. However, everything is not so rosy in the garden with regard to the state of health of the West's democratic institutions. With centralised federal lawmaking in the US and European Union (EU), there has been a tendency for larger commercial organisations to use lobbying and party-funding to influence legislation and effectively 'ace the market' by using regulation to create a virtual monopoly or to disenfranchise legitimate competition. This situation is exacerbated by the lack of regulation of political party financing and lobbying across almost all

Western nations. Political lobbying remains veiled in secrecy with most countries not even implementing or maintaining a registry of lobbyists.

Within Europe, whether real or not, there is a generally perceived democratic deficiency in the structure of EU lawmaking in Brussels. This deficiency coupled with political failure to address voter's concerns has fuelled growth in resentment of the policies of the European Commission and fuelled support for nationalist and anti-EU parties across the continent. In the UK, the vote for Brexit was an inevitable consequence. US lawmakers and parliamentarians across Europe are deeply unpopular; many deemed to be not living up to ethical standards of behaviour demanded by their voters. In the UK, the MPs' expenses scandal in 2009 was a symptom of wider corruption and has coloured UK politics and voters' views on MPs ever since. Even in the US, allegations of corruption and scandal have dogged Hilary Clinton's presidential campaign, and with voter antipathy toward her opponent Donald Trump, the 2016 US presidential race looks set for one of the lowest turnouts of recent years.

TI contends that across the EU there is high corruption risk in public procurement.[25] Legislative frameworks have been brought in line with EU procurement directives[26] intended to ensure fair, incorrupt tendering practices, but it is an open secret in many European countries that the rules are systematically circumvented with apparent impunity. It is not uncommon to see closed lists of 'approved suppliers', and published specifications in invitations to tender for national and local government projects amended post the tender deadline to favour a preferred supplier.

There is a public perception that protection is severely lacking for whistle-blowers who expose evidence of unethical conduct and criminality. This was evidenced from the 2014 indictment for breaching Swiss Bank secrecy laws, of the HSBC Private Bank whistle-blower, Hervé Falciani, who exposed the hidden bank accounts and earnings of

130,000 potential tax evaders in 2009. And as perceived by the revelations and US pursuit of National Security Agency (NSA) whistle-blower Edward Snowdon, who is widely lauded in the internet community as a libertarian hero.

So, with a wide perception in the public's mind across the Western world that their established politicians are corrupt, self-serving and deaf and blind to the concerns of the electorate, it's no wonder the voter antipathy toward the newly categorised political pariahs, the 'metropolitan elitists' has stimulated growth in support for disestablishmentarian politicians and parties. With an increasingly ethically minded populous and a ruling establishment rightly or wrongly deemed untrustworthy and corrupt, this provides for a very muddy canvas on which to paint a vision for an ethical enterprise or corporation. Given this long-running ground swell across the Western world, the political classes who can read the writing on the wall will inevitably fall into line with the public's zeitgeist. Others who don't will be cast on the scrapheap that is political failure. Consequently, legislatures will be forced to become more responsive to ethical issues and thus business ethics will be increasingly drawn to the front and centre of the political and business stage.

4. Avoiding the Snake Pit

4.1 In Business Dealings

If you are considering doing a business deal with a corporation or perhaps you're wanting to invest in or buy a firm or considering a merger, it's essential you know who and what you are dealing with. Vetting the background of a firm should be second nature if you want to sell to them or buy from them, so think how essential it must be to do the same screening if you're thinking of seeking employment with them. The last thing you need is to find yourself working in a firm a few months into your new position to find out it's an ethical Sodom and Gomorrah, with an egocentric psychopath for a boss. Or worse still, you might have invested a sizable amount of cash in an enterprise only to find out that while it's not a scam now, it's going to be one in six months' time due to the characters involved and the structures your new business partners are creating. So, a cardinal rule of staying out of the snake pit has to be 'do your 'due diligence' on more than just the hard assets and cash flow projections:

(1) **Characterise against profile of unethical corporations**: The literature has a plethora of examples of enterprises that have collapsed due to ethical failings and been wound up, and many times that number of organisations have been discredited by ethical scandals but survived. Examine the corporation for signs of 'malignancies'. Internal cultural signs such as 'mismatched employee values' and 'surveillance' issues can only be assessed if you have access to an internal source. But 'reputational degradation' and 'causing harm to others' are usually visible from outside the organisation. Remember the 'Duck' principle.

(2) **Characterise key individuals against psychopathic traits**: You don't have to be a clinical expert as you're not going to be

proffering a diagnosis or branding, labelling or confronting anyone with your findings. You simply require the ability to assess the behavioural traits of the person(s) you propose to do business with, as to whether someone is more likely to be High-P or not, and judge the comparative risk they would pose to you and your organisation. Most High-P individuals leave a trail of havoc in their wake, so above all check their pedigree, particularly regarding matters of trustworthiness and issues of moral turpitude. It's worth remembering the quote attributed to Albert Einstein: "*Whoever is careless with the truth in small matters cannot be trusted with important matters*".

(3) Conduct business risk assessment: Once you have judged 'who' and 'what' you are up against, you can make a comparative assessment of the hazards that they might pose to you and your organisation. A probabilistic assessment of those hazards becoming manifest is the measure of risk that you face.

4.2 In Employment Matters

If you are working for or with a High-P individual, their behaviour can make life hell or very interesting based on your proximity to them and perspective. High-P individuals are manipulative and exploitative, seeking to dominate and use others. If such a person sees you as useful, you might find that you've suddenly got a new very best friend. That is, just so long as they see you as useful, you don't come across as a threat and don't ever challenge their behaviour or authority. If being useful to a High-P co-worker suits your purpose then by all means cooperate and engage with them, but by no means think their friendliness toward you is a genuine friendship that will survive a time when you are no longer of use. And be especially careful that you are not drawn into unethical behaviour or set up to take the fall for the same. Remember that covering your arse with documentation to support the fact that you were squeaky clean will only go so far in the emotion of the fallout immediately after the 'shit hits the fan' and the High-P individual is taking no responsibility and blaming everyone else.

If you have a High-P co-worker and you are potentially competing for the next step up on the career ladder, you can expect plenty of psychological games and 'one-upmanship', including well-below-the-belt tactics. In larger organisations, there may be scope to move to a position or department where there are less challenging interpersonal relations. However, in such circumstance challenging the behaviour of a co-worker or manager or formally registering a 'conflict of personalities', though not uncommon in the work environment, is never a good career move. You should also consider that the High-P or unethical individual you have concerns over is in the organisation, because the organisation itself has become unethical and dysfunctional. In such circumstances and as a last resort, every individual pursuing a career should maintain an up-to-date CV. If you're in an uncomfortable or untenable position, it's best to take control into your own hands and manage the manner of your extrication from a difficult situation.

4.3 Don't Let It Happen to Your Firm

The ethical state of any organisation is a function of the cumulative effects of its internal decision-making by those senior executives in the driving seat. The influences on these executives are the stimuli of their rewards and punishments structure coupled with the bearing of personal character derived from learned behaviour and inherited traits. Such decision-making is set against the backdrop of corporate, industry and national culture, and the macroeconomic environment in which the corporation exists (see Figure 1).

Figure 1 – The Influences on Behaviour in Corporate Environment

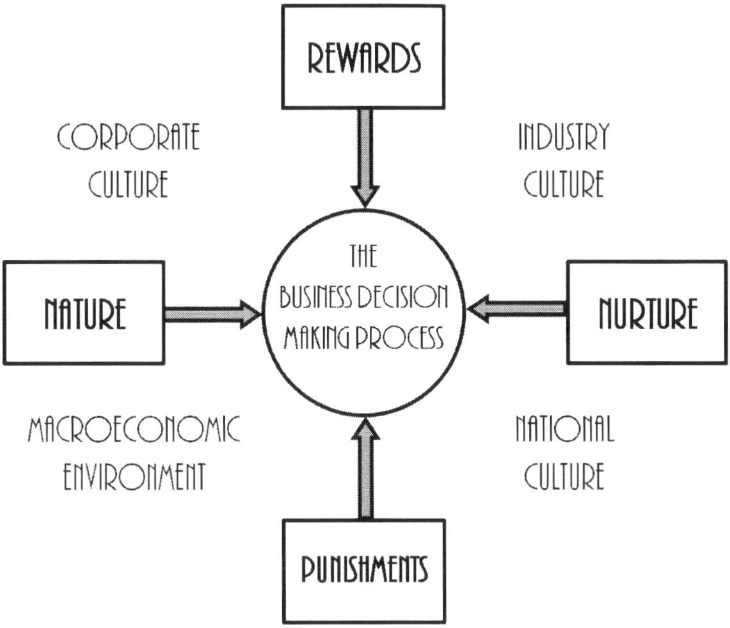

Any person, even a saint, can make an error of judgement, but multiple errors of judgement within the organisation can only be the result of individuals behaving dysfunctionally. To deal with this, actions can be taken on those aspects which influence decision-making that are within management's capacity to alter. In doing so, questions have to be answered when designing key management structures and systems as to what behaviour they will likely induce in those that are subject to them:

(1) **Reward and punishment structures**: For example, do short-term rewards, like this year's bonus being independent of all but this year's number on the bottom line, cause too great an emphasis on expedient decisions over best long-term outcomes? Do potential threats of punishments adversely impact managerial focus, such as a bank taking a director's home as collateral against a business loan? Rewards must be focussed on meeting the maximum value of the enterprise over its projected lifespan. If rewards focus on this year's figures alone, then the corporation's lifespan might not be much longer than that.

(2) **Corporate culture**: What attributes of behaviour are respected and rewarded in our firms? Does the firm reward and applaud those whom best serve it and those who uphold the values to which it aspires? Is the board's paradigm of its corporate culture (a) consistent with those of its industry and wider civil society, (b) framed in such a manner that it can be understood by all in the organisation, (c) accurately conveyed and understood at all levels in the organisation and (d) regularly reinforced and maintained at all levels?

(3) **Industry culture**: Do we promote our personnel's involvement with outside professional institutions that educate, expect and enforce professional standards of conduct? Do we conduct our business in accordance with commercial 'good faith', and standards of conduct deemed acceptable by commercial law codes?

(4) National culture: Do we conduct our business in accordance with standards of conduct deemed acceptable by wider civil society? Do we ally ourselves with other organisations that are in accord with the values of civil society?

(5) Governance, compliance and oversight: In addressing white-collar corporate crime and other unethical conduct, it is important to distinguish the different motivation and behavioural traits of 'leaders' and 'followers'. 'Followers' being much more susceptible to deterrence, by implementation of effective corporate governance, can be reduced in number through effective design of management reporting and compliance assurance systems. 'Followers' comprise the largest group of potentially dysfunctional individuals within the organisation. Therefore, reducing their numbers can only be beneficial, as whilst good governance does not deter 'leaders', owing to the complexity of the execution of corporate crime and other unethical conduct, 'leaders' largely carry out their dysfunctional behaviour aided, abetted and enabled by 'followers'.

(6) Effective leadership: Is our management good enough and do we have sufficient resources and the strength of character to deal with ethical challenges? Oversight in and of itself is not enough to prevent, detect and deal with criminal and unethical conduct within the organisation. Boards of directors should always be active and informed. They should have adequate size and capacity, with outside qualified expertise to undertake meaningful internal investigations and audits where necessary. In considering how companies should deal with cataclysmic corporate fraud issues, Bucy et al concluded:

"This points to one of the key insights from our study. The selection of the Board of Directors and corporate leadership should include individuals who have some experience and expertise in fraud deterrence and response. If not, corporate leadership will be ill-suited to guide the corporation through a potential crisis. On-the-job training or a circle-the-wagons approach, which is appropriate for other types of corporate crises, places at risk the existence of the corporation experiencing fraud."

Above all the board needs to believe that fraud exists; otherwise, they will not take steps to prevent it, and when it does occur, they will be incapable or unable to act appropriately. Too often nonexecutive directors are inactive on the part of the corporation on all but one day of the month, with nonexecutive directorships frequently treated as 'jollies' for old mates who are pals with the chairman or CEO. This group should be a key part of the board, bringing such expertise, experience and external objectivity to the board table at times of need, and thus Bucy et al observe:

"Only a sophisticated Board that is fully aware of the problems illegal activities can create for a company will be willing to implement these steps. Foot-dragging, delays, obfuscation, and confused leadership can prove fatal to a corporation."

(7) **Policy of dealing with wrongdoers**: There are several leadership issues that, though not unique to the British Isles, are peculiarly British in character. When unethical or criminal conduct is initially reported, detected or confirmed, the organisation can respond in a perverse manner with denial, prevarication, blame shifting and cover-up. How often in recent

UK criminal and ethical scandals has it been shown that the initial damage caused is insignificant to that wrought by the cover-up, and subsequent exposure thereof?

The Rotherham child abuse scandal and Hillsborough disaster are of particular note, with respectively the wholesale abuse and covering up of over 1,400 underage girls between 1997 and 2013, and the corporate manslaughter of 96 individuals in 1989, covered up by South Yorkshire Police for 26 years. Both cover-ups were deemed a price worth paying to avoid reputational damage and the protection of the careers of key executives and officers. The motives behind the cover-ups were *in the minds of the perpetrators* perfectly laudable and justifiable (had they not come to light). But such mind-bogglingly unethical acts of malfeasance in public office, so utterly futile, counterproductive and contrary to the public good were of such depth of depravity and scale that one has to form the opinion that these behaviours were not based on 'normal' rational thought processes. Put simply, where there are regulations but such weak leadership that there is no effective enforcement or penalty, there is no law and thus no deterrence. In the case of the Rotherham abuse scandal, the lack of timely action and the cover-up resulted in the continuation of child abuse on an almost industrial scale for a decade and a half.

Though not on the same scale, the same mechanics play out with other issues of crime and unethical conduct in the corporate environment for exactly the same motives. When a corporation discovers one of its own has behaved unethically and even defrauded the company, within the UK, corporate entities will in many cases sooner quietly terminate the culprit's employment and give them severance pay, preserved pension rights and even a reference if they 'go quietly', in order to not publicly impugn the managerial competence of the firm for allowing the problem to have occurred in the first place.

Another manifestation of what is the same basic problem of weak board administration is what I shall term the 'Sepp Blatter management style'. This is where the dysfunctional executive is effectively exposed, but he brazenly defends his blatant actions. The board, for the combination of the weakness of leadership and reluctance to enforce sanction, allows itself to fall victim to the persuasiveness of the miscreant's proposal that, "Yes, things went wrong, but only I can fix it". Thus, boards too often permit themselves to be talked into allowing the fox to reorganise the hen house after their rampage. What's the old saying? Fool me once shame on you, fool me twice… Within the UK, there is a trait for such 'Sepp Blatter-ism' within larger organisations, especially the NHS, where managerial failure is frequently tolerated, repeated and even rewarded with large pay-offs, or relocation into another NHS region at the same salary point – yet discharged bankrupts in wider industry and commerce are seldom allowed a second chance. Whereas in the US, the reverse is largely true with large-scale scammers frozen out of further high-level managements posts and discharged bankrupts regularly allowed a second chance.

Weak leadership in dealing with wrongdoers, however expedient, does nothing to prevent a reoccurrence of the same dysfunctional behaviour within the organisation or wider industry. Moreover, in a corporate environment, setting such a precedent by a weak managerial response to wrongdoing removes fear of the impact of exposure. This then emboldens others who would be 'leaders' and 'followers' alike. Thus, where no redemptive action is taken, the perpetrators of unethical conduct if either allowed to remain in post, relocated within a different division of the same firm or engaged in a new role with a new and unsuspecting employer, will repeat that same dysfunctional pattern of conduct.

(8) Human resources policy: Do we have the right human resource policy to support our corporate strategy? As with all divisional management, policy, tactics and culture need to be consistent with the overall corporate strategy of the organisation. After all, it's pointless differentiating your premium 'quality' brand product to be sold at high-end retailers in Bond Street if the operations strategy has the production department located in a third-world slum, the only focus of your purchasing department is to get prices down and human resources is intent on recruiting back-alley spivs for the sales department. It should be self-evident that if implementation policies are inconsistent with overall corporate strategy, goals will be missed and the only place you'll be selling your not-so 'premium goods' is down the Old Kent Road.

Financial motivations and even the need to finance drug addiction have been cited as motivations by corporate thieves and fraudsters. Do we motivate the best behaviour by reward both through monetary means and recognition of service? It stands to reason that if you expect an honest day's work for a job, you should pay honest and fair wages. Additionally, line managers need to be cognisant of the personal welfare as well as the health and safety of their employees, not least for the reason that they have a fiduciary duty to them within the workplace. As such, a degree of empathy with one's subordinates and colleagues is essential in spotting issues of emotional, mental and financial stress, especially in relation to drug abuse or alcoholism.

Do we identify those who, if placed in a sensitive position, by their nature might pose a hazard to the organisation? If you need people to manage or turn around an organisation, and manage it in an ethical and sustainable way, then your human resource policy needs to be consistent with the same. To that end, placing a High-P individual in a position of influence is a high-risk action. If ethics and sustainability of the enterprise are of secondary concern, then the appointment of a High-P CEO might just fit the bill. However, if this choice is made, the organisation might well have crossed the Rubicon on a one-way trip to short to medium-term success or damnation.

Babiak and Hare give a good overview of psychopath's behaviour in the workplace and I would recommend their work, *Snakes in Suits: When Psychopaths Go to Work,*[27] not only for commercial professionals but for those who are intent on a career in regulatory enforcement. Whilst there are many methods of personnel selection, each being suited to differing organisational cultures, none is wholly perfect in filtering out High-P individuals. In jobs, professional and organisational cultures that don't provide the opportunity for High-P individuals to excise their desire for narcissism, there is little risk that such individuals will even apply, but for senior executive and CEO positions the risk is real. In their chapter entitled "Enemy at the Gates" Babiak and Hare illuminate many practical ways of screening out potential High-P individuals during personnel selection. Basically, the crux of the process is to seek to differentiate between the High-P charismatic and transformational style behaviour of the candidate, much of which we have alluded to earlier in this text, and bearing in mind that the High-P individual will be prone to exaggerate and even be an adept liar. They may even have achieved prior career success, albeit at the expense of others left trailing in their wake, and may even come with a good reference from their prior employer, who is glad to see the back of them.

An experienced human resource professional will tell you that they can easily spot a charismatic High-P psychopath from a transformational leader. I would beg to differ; after all, High-P individuals can be accomplished liars and very persuasive. I well recall an experience of being interviewed for a senior marketing position within a large chemicals group in the UK. The newly appointed group human resources director gave me the corporate spiel and described to me the qualities in the marketing professional they were seeking and expressed his desire that I perform a ten-point psychometric test. They placed great merit in this test and he assured me that within the space of 30 minutes of me commencing to answer the questions he would have a thorough understanding of my personal characteristics. The questions on two sheets of A4 seemed too few to gain such insight and perhaps tactlessly I noted that to him. He assured me it was fantastically accurate and that they used it to select all their best executives, one of whom from earlier in our discussion turned out to be personally known to me, and he had been described by the HRD as one of the best managing directors in the group. I duly completed the test and sat back to listen to the rough, but not necessarily unflattering, assessment of my personal qualities. I could do nought but smile at even at some of the inaccuracies of so rough a test, much to the HRD's annoyance. I think he perceived that I wasn't taking it seriously, and it was true. I wasn't. He had accurately perceived that at least. My amusement came for the fact that the man they described as one of their 'best' and by whose standard they were trying to recruit similar individuals, I knew as an unreformed alcoholic, fraudster and convicted tax evader who had all the personal traits of a High-P individual.

Thankfully, I wasn't offered the position, and wouldn't have taken it if I was, as they might have sent me to work for a drunken fraudster. As for the company, understandably such an organisation was unable to withstand the harsh realities of commerce and the group was bought out and broken up shortly thereafter.

Regarding the abilities of human resource professionals and board members to filter out High-P individuals, I think that the litany of catastrophic corporate failures and ethical scandals and the role of High-P individuals in them stand as stark evidence to the failings if not a damning indictment of the shortcomings and subjectivity in personnel selection processes. In 1999 the world's leading head-hunters and HR professionals teamed up to write the book *Lessons from the Top: The Search for America's Best Business Leaders*[28], which profiled 50 leading US executives and held them out to be the crème de la crème, and role models to be emulated. Within just a few years three of them, Kenneth Lay (Enron), Dennis Kozlowski (Tyco) and Bernie Ebbers (Worldcom) would be in jail for fraud and a further three would be collectively fined over US$20 million for fraudulent practices. So next time you discuss profiling with a HR professional, bear in mind the pedigree of their profession. No matter what the best human resources people tell you, such selection processes are only ever 50% right at getting best fit first time around, yet HR never seem to have a Plan B in the form of a substitute on the bench. It is also worth noting that when things do go wrong with ethics in corporations, the problem commenced with a poor appointment or trust and authority placed in the hands of the wrong person.

* * *

5. Bear Traps in Commerce

Commerce is simply the act of buying and selling goods or services within a market. Whether just business services or goods for raw materials or resale, corporations need to buy something to which they add value and trade, and this is the *raison d'être* of business. So, it's not unreasonable to infer that every organisation employs someone who fulfils the function of buyer and seller. Buying and selling can be viewed as different roles on the same gameboard. Both require similar types of skilled and commercially savvy people who need to know their market and can discern and communicate the values in the product or services transacted. They also must understand their counterpart's role. Correctly conducted under 'perfect market' conditions the roles of the buyer and seller are 'symbiotic'.

Under nominal 'perfect market' conditions, economics will determine which one of several suppliers of substitute products wins business and grows market share. A *'product'* in marketing terms can be defined as consisting of *'a bundle of characteristics'* which are deemed to be the product's qualities.[29] The choice to purchase is driven by the weighting of these product qualities and other factors such as availability, delivery time and critically the price, i.e. 'what', 'when' and 'how much'. In a quality driven market, the 'what' is the key determinant of utility in the eyes of the customer, with each characteristic of the product contributing to its overall perceived value. It is the comparison of product quality with other market substitutes that governs the price the customer is prepared to pay and whose product is brought.

When it comes to a market commodity, with a dozen different potential suppliers, the key market determinants come down to 'when' and 'how much'. In such markets, it's critical to reduce the length of supply chain from supplier to buyer to minimise time and cost, i.e. the 'when' and 'how'. In truly price-sensitive markets, buyers won't usually consider moving supply or requesting re-quotations inside a price fluctuation range of ±3% but will be susceptible to move above it. If buyers detect a deviation of +5% in the cost of his supply relative to the market mean, they will definitely move. Where the buyer's price is 3% below the market norm, he may expect his supplier to renegotiate price, and at 5% below the supplier will definitely renegotiate. Sellers will usually have an advantage over the buyer in terms of market intelligence, in that the buyer must look to the external market to measure the mean price of the commodity, but may not necessarily have the market network to do so. The salesman will have that market network plus the added pressure from his company's finance team to get his prices moved up in line with their increasing production costs.

Under 'imperfect market' conditions, the normal economics of the market break down or become subverted. This occurs in circumstances where there are too few players for the normal balancing rules of competition to apply. Such circumstances only exist where the seller has a virtual monopoly, a market where there are no realistic substitutes available. Effectively the seller can abuse that monopoly power to charge as much as the would-be buyer, within constraints, can afford to meet the need for the product.

Legitimate monopolies include:

(1) Exclusive control of the factors of production: For example, where the marginal costs of the means of production are high, through the need for significant capital investment or technology, such as in telecommunications or fibre-optic internet infrastructure.

(2) Patent right or copyrights in the production of a good or service: For example, for patents, these grant a limited period of exclusive commercial exploitation (usually 20 years in most jurisdictions, but extendible in some circumstances) for the owner of the patent right. In the UK, copyright protection extends from the time the work is made public for 50 years thereafter. In the US for works published after 1922, but before 1978, these are protected for 95 years from the date of publication. If the work was created, but not published, before 1978, the copyright lasts for the life of the author plus 70 years.

(3) Government regulation: For example, land rights (such as mining rights and other rights to exploit natural resources, such as water or fishing, or wavelength broadcasting licenses) and obscurely, titles by letters patent. Governments can also retain exclusivity on control of certain goods and services in the national interest. Governments seldom create a monopoly for the benefit of private individuals or companies, generally being constrained by multinational agreements on creation of monopolies. However, they remain vulnerable to pressure and undue influence from lobbyists and political party funders to institute the same. Using regulation to create a virtual monopoly or disenfranchise legitimate competition is frequently referred to as 'acing the market'.

(4) Network and distribution economies of scale: In a market where new entrants would require high capital investment and instant high volume sales to compete, there is a virtual monopoly that is created by economies of scale. An example would be in microprocessor production by companies such as Intel whose product is so widely used in personal computers that it has massive advantage through economies of scale.

(5) Natural monopolies: For example, where a rare mineral is only found in limited geographic territories and commercial exploitation is thus limited. Examples are Wolfram, the ore of tungsten (used in high-output lighting and speciality hard alloys), where 92% of the world's mine production lies within eastern Asia and more specifically 83% in China, or Coltan, the principal ore of tantalum (an essential metal used in mobile phone electronics), where 80% of world production is located in the Democratic Republic of the Congo.

Illegitimate monopolies include:

(1) Monopolies created by merger: Where two or more large players in a market propose to combine, wherein the newly created entity would be able to exert a monopoly power over consumers, particularly with regard to restricting choice and wherein regulatory authorities may deem that merger is contrary to the public good. In commercial terms, such entities rarely pass regulatory examination, but some do come into being, when the regulator is insufficiently motivated or stimulated to act.

(2) Cartels: Groups of suppliers to a market, who formally or informally collude for the purpose of creating artificial monopoly conditions by controlling supply or fixing prices and thereby restricting competition. As such, cartels usually fall foul of national and international antitrust legislation, save where founded under international agreements between nationally sovereign bodies, and even if successful, their action on the market being unsustainable, means they are short-lived. However, the Organization of the Petroleum Exporting Countries (OPEC) is a textbook cartel founded in 1960 and still in existence today, probably due to its long-term ineffectiveness in controlling world oil prices. In 2015 OPEC countries accounted for only 37% of world oil output and 20% of world gas output, large but insufficient to affect monopoly supply conditions on the market.

(3) Illegitimate government monopolies: Government-held monopolies deemed in contradiction of international treaty or national or supranational constitutional courts. For example, the Italian government's retention of monopoly on job placement services which was ruled 'illegitimate' by the European Courts in 1998.

(4) Criminal monopolies: Excluding collusion between criminals, and criminal organisations for the purposes of supply of illegal contraband or the execution of crime, criminal organisations can create effective monopolies by threats of violence, intimidation, blackmail or bribery, over entire otherwise legitimate but limited market sectors in limited geographic regions. For example, the 'Camorra' control of the toxic and municipal waste disposal industry in Naples from 2008 to 2015.[30, 31]

By their very nature, monopolies are difficult to compete with. Unless the penny hasn't dropped yet, that's why they are formed, to stifle or preclude competition. Patent protection is a form of limited legitimate monopoly to reward the inventor for his novel contribution to industrial utility. Copyright is a limited legitimate monopoly to reward a creator of original works for their lifetime and that of their immediate heirs, and natural resource rights are reward for an individual or enterprise who exploits that resource in exchange for a royalty return to the state. Rights granted under legitimate monopolies can be legally defended and enforce in the civil courts.

In some circumstances, it's possible to legitimately break a legitimate monopoly. This can be done by legally circumventing or successfully challenging a granted patent or by lobbying for legislative change to dissolve and established government monopoly. This occurred with the deregulation of state-owned monopolies in UK under the Thatcher administration in the 1980s.

Breaking a legitimate monopoly by illegitimate means, such as copyright piracy, is uniquely for intellectual property law, subject to criminal sanction. In this circumstance, judicial action and sanction is not justified by the state on the grounds that the rights of the copyright holder were violated, and as such, a dispute would have to be resolved by a civil action. The perpetrators of the sale or supply of counterfeit copyright goods are prosecuted under consumer goods legislation for supply of goods that are wrongly described or unfit for purpose. Governments are motivated to vigorously enforce copyright infringement as copyrighted products of the creative industries, such as music, film and computer gaming as well as famous branded designer goods are 'Big Business', and these industries are major contributors to government revenues, not to mention that they are also 'Big Lobbyists' of government. Consider this: The UK's creative industry in 2015 was worth in excess of £71 billion, accounting for 5.2% of the UK economy. Hollywood accounted for US$504 billion and 3.2%

of US GDP and all US TV, music and film accounted for US$913 billion. In 2014, India's Bollywood accounted for US$7.5 billion and 0.5% of Indian GDP.

Illegitimate monopolies are even harder to compete against as by their definition, they are usually illegal and constructed by unethical individuals and criminals, who will be predisposed to use unethical and criminal means to defend their illegitimate business interests or 'market ownership' and are likely do so as eagerly as governments defend their legitimate monopolies. Inconveniently, illegitimate monopolies are not advertised or conveniently stamped 'Copyright ©' or 'Patent Pending'. If they were, such criminally contrive entities would attract the attention of regulators.

An illegitimate monopoly market when put under scrutiny of a detailed market analysis, for example when profiled according to 'Porter's Five forces'[32] might appear as Figure 2 below:

Figure 2 – An illustrative Illegitimate Monopoly Market and Porter's Five Forces

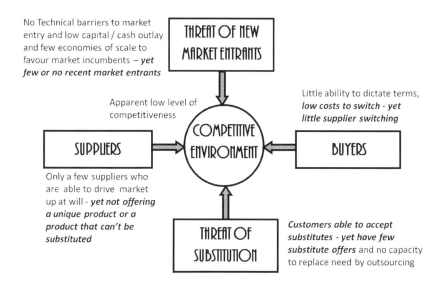

Supplier Power: Few organisations operating as a cartel or even just a single supplier who can drive the market up at will, yet not offering a unique product or offering a product that can be substituted.

Buyer Power: Very low levels of product switching. Buyers paying high prices with apparently little power or option or choice to substitute supply or dictate terms – yet buyers have comparatively low costs of switching and low switching rates.

Competitive Rivalry: Few competitors in the market – yet those don't necessarily have a monopoly supply position or low-cost base for their product.

Threat of Substitution: Despite an ability to accept substitutes, typically the customers have few offers of substitutes to the product that are not identical or similar in performance. Neither can they outsource the production using the product, outside the affected market.

Threat of New Entry: Apparently few barriers to entering the market and few significant economies of scale to advantage the existing market dominating suppliers – yet few or no recent new market entrants.

The imperfect market profile generated by the illegitimate monopoly would create the following commercial conditions: from the perspective of the incumbent seller, the market is highly profitable and they would obviously wish to maintain the status quo. However, from the perspective of buyers, they have a problem of high price relative to the quality of the goods and consequential dissatisfaction with value for money. Buyers, if presented with a viable substitute or alternative product supply on better terms (and without fear of the consequences), would take it. They also have a problem from an economic perspective; the relationship between the seller and buyer has become 'parasitic'. As with most parasitized hosts, ultimately if pressed too hard they will die. Generally the decline is slow and insidious over many years, with no apparent symptoms followed by the apparent sudden collapse and succumbing to the parasite's effects. In commercial terms, the buyer's business would become less competitive with others selling substitute products against them, or indeed uncompetitive against other competitors who can source raw materials from outside the illegitimate monopoly. They would gradually turn from making profits to losses, and when these economic circumstances can no longer be tolerated or sustained, that's when the symptoms become evident with increasing urgent rounds of cost cutting and redundancies. If business turnaround strategies fail, the spiral of decline results in commercial death and closure of the firm. It's for these reasons that illegitimate monopolies created by cartels and others are economically unstable with a tendency to be short-lived. However, 'short-lived' in commercial terms can be years to a decade. When it eventually occurs, the decline of the illegitimate monopoly market is typified by an apparently sudden collapse of the whole market sector, within a geographic region usually within a few months to a few years or the sudden sharp stepwise decline in the sellers' price when the monopoly is broken as the product reverts back to being a commodity. If the monopoly doesn't die through the killing of its hosts, breaking of the monopoly is brought about by either intervention of a regulator or successful entry into the market by a new supplier breaking the blockade.

From the perspective of a potential new and naïve entrant to the market, the commercial opportunity seems on the face of it attractive, with apparently weak lethargic competitors and high market prices and margins. To the sceptical and cynical, wizened by age and swollen of liver from drinking too long at the well of wisdom, when you see the symptoms of the imperfect market conditions accompanied by the apparent 'invisibility' of the crucial monopoly forming barrier to external competition in the form of regulation, license, patent or product production advantages or economies of scale of the competition, the situation becomes more complex. An illegitimate monopoly market will have many of the following characteristics:

- Operate outside 'perfect market' rules.

- Is economically unstable.

- Is an effective monopoly but not obvious to regulators.

- Has hidden barriers to entry that enables the monopoly.

- Has fewer sellers (a cartel) or a dominant seller who is likely the 'market owner'.

- The market owner maintains the status quo by deterring or resisting new market entrants.

- Monopoly breakdown causes a sharp collapse in the market price for the product.

- Or, if not broken, results in slow insidious weakening ending in apparently quick 'commercial death' of the buyers' firm or market sector.

If you've come across a market that has a few lethargic competitors, high profitability and few apparent barriers to entry, you've serendipitously found a hidden gem of a market, or come across a functioning illegitimate monopoly, potentially the domain of a cartel or criminal organisation, and a veritable 'bear trap' of a market to enter. How bad a bear trap and whether the market is worth entering depends upon just how big and nasty the jaws of the trap are and what the potential rewards will be for the likely pain. Consider that the unethical founders of the illegitimate monopoly will react both commercially and otherwise to maintain the status quo of their market ownership and control. Even if you successfully enter the market and effectively break the owner's monopoly, the product's price will decline and revert to being driven by 'perfect market' economics. *At some point one must learn not all opportunities are there to be taken.* To underline the point, there are probably massive profits to be made in municipal refuse collection and waste disposal in Naples, but do you really want to bid for the business against the incumbent contractors?

5.1 The Problem with Selling

As any salesman will tell you, sales is a high-pressure job. Most sales teams are target driven with specific targets being levied not just on the team but on every member. Team managers use every motivational method imaginable, from gimmicks to prizes for the best to personal humiliation of the month's weakest performer on the team, but for the salesman, the biggest draw has to be 'commission'. Commissions and the capacity to far exceed a flat basic pay play a major role in the salesman's life. I should know, I spent 15 years in a sales management role where my pay was 100% commission based, and that commission was only assessed on goods that were paid for.[33] While I had no cap on potential earnings, quite simply, if I didn't sell, my family didn't eat and I could lose the roof over our heads. Furthermore, I had to meet all my own travel costs and if the customer didn't pay up, I was liable for the cost of any lost goods. The nature of the job by its potential rewards and punishments taught me marketing focus and how to choose where I could realistically sell. Above all, it taught me how to ascertain those accounts where I would meet indomitable competition, and how to identify a corrupt buyer who would not buy from me at any price … or worse … wouldn't pay up, or at least not on time.

Pressures to perform are reflected in the job's high turnover rates and often by executive burnout, especially the further up the greasy pole you climb in sales management. Given this pressure, where substantial contracts are up for grabs or where there is a large parcel of business with a single account to be retained, sales management will understandably be highly motivated to seize or guard what they view as 'key account business'. Given that such big potential rewards are there for the seller, the buyer is usually in a strong position, assuming he has competitive market offers. If you have an unethical seller, and given the numbers of High-P individuals in senior commercial management, it's highly likely evens odds that one out of five or six of your competitor's CEO's is a High-P individual who is predisposed to resort to unethical means to win and retain key account business. As a medium-sized competitor at the quality end of our market, I had long since learned that were it came to such sized accounts I could compete on price with my competitors, on a like-for-like basis if there was a level playing field. I could not compete if the playing field had been corrupted. The essential problem was that if a buyer was corruptible through the inducement of a highly motivated seller they would just as likely buy from whoever offered the biggest backhander. Thus, if you played that game you'd likely get embroiled in a bidding war. If you're only a middle-ranking player and you enter that game, the guy with the deepest pockets will outbid you. If he's a bigger player in the market he will use his market clout against you. Whatever the size of the organisation intent on winning and retaining business by such means, the costs employed to implement the economically unstable and illegitimate monopoly will be such that the overall net margin for the business is frequently not worth the effort – long term. This was particularly a problem in my position having to cover costs of sales. Over and above this problem, it could potentially kill my would-be customer's business, and in business, as in life, dead men pay no bills. Thus, with certain accounts, I learned it was imprudent to attempt entry unless they had properly policed procurements systems in place. At other non-key accounts where I attempted to sell but the buyer was acting irrationally according to economic principles in paying more for inferior goods or service, I'd just have to walk away.

Having considered the motivational forces at play influencing why a seller can induce a buyer to be corrupt, how can we recognise the signs and guard against the possibility of corruption? The answer is in the normal mechanics of relationships and how that relationship can become abusive. The relationship between buyer and seller has to be one of mutual trust, which results in the meeting of minds over an offer, a commitment to buy and a promise to supply at an agreed price. Repeated purchasing and supplying by the same individuals strengthens that relationship of trust. It's generally easier to develop that relationship if the parties are friendly toward one another. To that end the salesman is informally taught by older hands skills in the trade to develop such skills in cordiality and rapport. Whether selling nationally or internationally, in my opinion, a friendly cheery disposition and an ability to discuss football, cricket, sport in general, food, culture or even the ability to entertain, to share a meal with your clients, or get drunk together, even to the point of being able to get up and sing in a karaoke bar are all essential aspects of the salesman's role for developing rapport. Over my career, all the best salesmen I met had these skills and focused at least as much in selling themselves as the product; it was their personal reputation and trustworthiness in the eyes of the buyers that underlined the product sales literature and company warranties. To develop such accord between seller and buyer, it is normal practice in most industries to give small gifts: desk scatter gifts, a pen, card holder, desk diaries, etc. At Christmas, a bottle of Scotch and a shared meal or drink is all par for the course. To this point everything would be deemed acceptable in most markets, with the sums expended on the buyer being deemed to be too insignificant to induce corruption. However, what about when the gifts get a little more expensive and the shared meals become free nights out on the town, periodic complimentary weekend-away breaks for the buyer and their partner, a large hamper or gift tokens at Christmas? At some point there has to be a transition between a casual perk of the job and a greedy indulgence. This is the point where a motivated and unethical seller will test the ethics and resolve of the buyer. The corrupt seller usually doesn't send its salesman to the buyer with a brazen offer and a wad of notes in a brown paper envelope. Real events are subtler and nuanced as the seller is keen not to get their face slapped by rejection. Where a motivated corrupt seller sees a potentially compliant buyer, it will usually make an approach away from the buyer's place of work, in an informal setting where the buyer feels at ease and is removed from the symbols and trappings of the buyer's firm that might induce pangs of torn loyalty, guilt or fear of discovery. Such settings might be the seller's annual golf tournament for their clients, held on one of those free weekend breaks at a country park hotel, or a corporate sponsored day at the races, with lots to eat and drink and maybe a complimentary allowance to place bets. Usually it's the salesman's boss who does the final sounding out of the buyer's feelings for his firm, whether they feel properly rewarded and recognised for efforts and are potentially pliable: *"Shocked you never got that promotion, mate, you're worth more than their paying you"*, *"So, what's next for you? You know you're never going to get further up the greasy pole than you already are at that firm"*, *"Shocking the amount we pay in taxes, isn't it"*, *"Sometimes it's nice just to kick-back and enjoy things; you deserve it and we appreciate you"*, *"So, kids off at University now, that's going to cost"*. Depending on the signals that come back from the buyer, the subtly worded, almost casual inducement is pitched; *"Perhaps we might be able to help you there, after all what goes around comes around, and isn't that what friends are for? ..."*

Whilst the scenario painted is largely fictitious, the underlying mechanisms of 'why' and 'how' the buyer-seller relationship is formed, maintained, and in some circumstances, degraded and abused by unethical conduct is essentially the same. The key challenge for the ethical organisation has to be how to maintain the essential aspects of the buyer-seller relationship without allowing its debasement, and how to detect whether your buyer has turned to the 'dark side' should the worst already have happened.

The first line of defence should be set limits for on what is, and isn't acceptable corporate hospitality for your purchasing team. Many firms impose a cash limit of circa £25 on commercial gifts. Any offer of a gift beyond that must be rejected and reported. Some companies pool the buyers' gifts and raffle them at Christmas. All hospitality given and received should be properly logged and recorded as 'entertainment expense, given and received'. Making the same transparent and a function of the contract of employment sets proper policeable bounds, and serves notice as to what behaviour the organisation deems is acceptable conduct from its employees and what is not. In general, it's not wise to let your buyers attend large corporate social events held by sellers, especially if they are not accompanied by other senior staff. If a buyer has been turned, then unless they're stupid this can be hard to detect and prove. Illicit payments are not necessarily made in cash. In one case I knew of, the miscreant was rewarded by having his annual golf club fees of several thousand pounds paid for him. What made it stick out was the fact that co-workers came to know he was a member of the most prestigious club in the area and with fees equating to more than 10% of his take-home pay, they wondered how he could afford it. Gossip of the same type was caused when a sourcing manager working in a warehousing environment, away from commercial oversight, routinely wore designer suits and shoes to work. When the person's performance was subsequently scrutinised, the party was purchasing some services at a mark-up of 100%. Others, who had their illicit commissions paid into overseas accounts and went annually to pick them up in cash, were much harder to detect, were it not for the obviously economically unstable monopoly that they generated and tried to irrationally defend. When a buyer tells his sales director that he's purchasing a commodity raw material at 30–40% over market price for strategic reasons and declines to elucidate what they are, then there's clearly something wrong somewhere.

Allowing your sales team to be corrupt by inciting and paying bribes is a twin-edged sword. You might win and retain business (at a cost) but the actual payers of the bribes can start to think, "Well, what about me", particularly if they are High-P individuals. One such salesperson I knew was known in our trade as Maurice 'eight percent'. By his own admission to me, he had been, let's say, 'in charge of certain funds' kept offshore for payment of promotional services for his company. Though he didn't like the fact, he obtained his nickname through offering very attractive prices to certain agents and paying them a handsome 8% commission, which at the time, equated to almost the profit cut retained by the manufacturing division of his employer. Normal commissions in our trade were 3–5%. In Maurice's case, his commissions had a boomerang element. Eight percent was given out, but 3% came back to him personally via a third party. It was a quality in Maurice that his employer didn't appreciate, leading to his enforced early retirement, on a generous pension, of course. The problem is once an organisation sanctions unethical conduct and gets sloppy in managing its employees' behaviour in any of its operations or divisions, it's practically impossible to prevent contagion spreading to other parts of the organisation. There simply isn't any firewall effective against this type of infection, and unless promptly excised, the negative behaviour will become culturally engrained and systemic. Maurice's old company had an efficient and well-designed, large-capacity manufacturing facility, and I can say with some degree of expertise it was the lowest-cost manufacturing facility of its type in the world from the day it opened to the day they closed it. I know; I toured the site on more than one occasion with operations experts from India. In addition, even though it was based in Europe, due to its simple and elegant design with fairly unsophisticated automation, its manpower costs were less than 5% of product sales price as compared to 7% for its closest competitor in India. Under normal circumstances the industry's raw materials costs equated to 50–65% of end-market product prices. Yet the problem was their purchasing department were on a like-for-like basis paying 30–40% above market rates paid by its Indian competitors for commodity raw materials. Additionally, they were buying them primarily through one middleman rather than direct from the sources of manufacture. Why? I leave you to join the dots …

In the Anglo-Saxon economies, any part of the process of offering, soliciting or paying of bribes is generally a criminal offence. It is also a criminal offence if the buyer is a public official in any OECD country. Furthermore, it exposes the selling organisation to the possibility of civil action for inducing malfeasance in all jurisdictions. Criminal penalties can be a few years in prison or unlimited fines, with the present record standing a US$1.4 billion in the TeliaSonera case, and in countries like China, it can result in a penalty of life imprisonment or being shot.

5.2 The Problem with Buying

The sales team of any organisation, perhaps with the assistance of an agency distribution network, are responsible for selling the entire corporation's turnover in product, whereas buyers will be responsible for purchasing 50–75% of the equivalent value of the company's turnover in purchased goods and services. Sales managers will outnumber buyers by between five and six to one. So, by virtue of their being responsible for a greater total value of goods transacted, it can reasonably be argued that a purchasing manager has greater capacity to positively influence the value added of the company's product sold, and thus have greater potential impact on the company's profit margin. A typical sales manager in the UK will have a salary in excess of £40,000, plus commission, plus fringe benefits, with associate expense account and company car, and have every expectation of one day rising up the greasy pole to become a sales and marketing director. Yet his counterpart, the purchasing manager, experience for experience, will typically earn a 6% lower salary, with fewer fringe benefits, and will generally have less opportunity to reach the boardroom. So even coming from a background of sales and marketing, I think it fair to say that the role of purchasing manager is generally underappreciated and under rewarded relative to their value to the company.

5.2.1 Blinkered and Lazy Buyers

In comparison to a competitive dog-eat-dog career in sales, purchasing managers are usually less commercially proficient than their counterparts in sales. Even in today's business world with the ever-increasing standardisation of business requirements for ISO 9001, 14001 and 18001, there are some organisations where the purchasing manager never leaves the office to visit or indeed vet his suppliers but simply relies on the visiting salesman to 'tick the boxes' on the supplier assessment questionnaire. At worst, the buyer e-mails it to his supplier overseas and receives the duly completed form by return. These forms provide no evidence that the supplier performs his duties to the required standard and provides no assurance that the goods supplied are manufactured to appropriate standards and under appropriate conditions or are otherwise fit for purpose. As for warranty, with what is it guaranteed and backed up by? Such tick-box questionnaires are totally useless other than to meet a perceived bureaucratic need for a document to be generated, or to act as a psychological crutch for the buyer, who when things go wrong can absolve themselves of blame by saying: *"Well, the supplier told me they complied. Look, I have it on paper in black and white."* Such forms do nothing to prevent unethical suppliers just ticking the box and otherwise being declared ethical and compliant suppliers. The only thing that will do is for the buyer to get off their behind and, with appropriately technically qualified staff if required, visit the suppliers' facilities at a time of the buyer's choosing to conduct a thorough audit. The reason buyers don't like this approach is that ultimately it is they who would have to approve the supplier. Effectively the buyer is the person taking responsibility for doing business with the seller. Allowing sellers to self-audit by tick-box forms rather than the buyer conducting a supplier site audit equates to ineffective supplier screening by sloppy buyers.

A buying manager's job is about evaluating and approving new suppliers and products, ensuring ongoing compliance of the established approved suppliers and delisting poor ones. These functions are effectively purchasing 'network development and maintenance' and they are strategically necessary. A buying manager's job is also about working with the organisation's master scheduler to place purchase orders such that the goods arrive on time for processing with minimal cost implications for inbound inventory. These 'routine processing' aspects of the buyer's work are also an essential role but largely tied to operations. I have found that where the buying manager is located within the organisation greatly influences the balance of how they perform their role, whether toward 'routine processing' or 'development and maintenance'. Where the buyer is integrated wholly into operations, reporting to the production director, the buyer reverts almost exclusively to a purchasing clerical role. Whereas, if integrated into the commercial team and reporting to the principal commercial director, even though in both positions in the organisation the buyer will still take their demand lead from the master scheduler, the buyer will become more exposed to the wider commercial environment and purchasing strategy becomes better integrated into the whole organisation.

I encountered a small-scale but perfect example of a lazy buying department when I worked for Amersham International at their facilities in Cardiff back in the eighties. My lab needed a new shelving system to house and organise our growing collection of speciality chemicals. On complaining about the issue to my boss, he said, *"Perfect project for you. You want it changed? Sort it."* I duly discussed the issue with my colleagues, browsed through the catalogues of several local suppliers and identified a viable system of shelving and product containment, and with requisition in hand I popped down to the purchasing department. At the almost caricature hatch in the wall counter reminiscent of a British Rail ticket booth, I slid my requisition through the slot. The clerk's expression looked ominous. Peering over her glasses she said, *"Hmmm, I don't think we can do this; the company you want is not on the approved suppliers list."* Adding, *"Better leave it* with us and well get back to you." A few days later my boss got a call and nonplussed he called me into his office. *"That shelving system you wanted, it's going to cost £3,000 just to get the quotes."* *"Don't be silly,"* I replied. *"That's more than the costs of the shelves and there are six firms in Cardiff within five miles that can do what we need, and quotes are free."* To which was the answer, *"But they're not on the approved suppliers list."* Amersham International had originally started out as the government's Radio-Chemical Centre at Amersham in Buckinghamshire. It was originally part of the UK Civil Service before its floatation and operated a civil service procurement system. To get a quote you simply had to be on the list. The company had only moved to Cardiff some four years prior but all approved suppliers were still located in Buckinghamshire. Purchasing claimed that all the approved suppliers would charge for the 300-mile round-trip and the time involved to measure up for the quote. Miffed to say the least, I returned to the hatch in the wall. A new face appeared at the window, a young girl fairly new to the company. I politely enquired how I could get a supplier approved. She said she'd check and went away. A few minutes later, she returned and said, *"To get on the suppliers list you have to have supplied the company."* *"That's perfect,"* I replied with a smile while in reality thinking: Oh Christ! I'd fallen through a crack in reality and landed on the Vogon home world from *Hitchhiker's Guide to the Galaxy*. Thinking quickly and trying it on, I handed over my requisition and said, *"Can you just make out a quotation request for this shelf supplier?"* She casually responded, *"Are they on the approved suppliers list?"* *"I'm absolutely almost positive,"* I replied vaguely but in a confident manner, while thinking, they will be just as soon as you fill out the bloody purchase order. Comforted by my assurances, the young girl processed the quote request to the local company. A few days later a guy from the local shelving company arrived. I collected him from the reception and accompanied him to our lab where he commenced to measure up. *"I'll be 30 minutes, mate,"* he said. *"I'll call you when I'm done."* *"Sorry I can't leave you alone in this lab. We work* with radio-chemicals and other hazardous stuff," I replied. I stood by while he measured up and safely escorted him off the premises. He faxed in a very competitive price indeed, saying he'd been trying to get in the door with our firm for years. My boss, who was now well pleased, confirmed the quote was acceptable. Lo and behold our shelving system arrived within the week and was installed to the satisfaction of all concerned. A couple of weeks later and on my coffee break, I passed the local shelving guy in the corridor, strolling along unattended as if he were an employee of the site. *"Thought I saw you off the premises a week ago!"* I said. Grinning from ear-to-ear with both thumbs up he replied, *"Amazing! I've been here every other day for the last fortnight, and now I'm just in measuring for a big contract with engineering."* The man did a roaring trade. Our company had four years plus of pent-up demand and engineering components stored on pallets on the deck rather than in racking, because department heads were reluctant to pay three grand for a quote. Now unbeknown to this little firm, they had their own mini-monopoly, being the only approved supplier of shelving to that site within 150 miles!

A ludicrous little vignette you might think, but consider this: there are departments of national and local government which still purchase in the same way, even for major multi-million-pound engineering contracts. A typical example of these being the UK MoD and US DoD, where UK, DEF-STAN and US, MIL-D specifications in procurement for products are still used that have been long since superseded in wider industry by health and safety laws, simply because it takes decades for such government organisations to change their procurement standards and approve new suppliers.

Approving a supplier can be time-consuming and costly. Being let down badly by a supplier due to faulty goods unfit for purpose, or goods that don't arrive, can be even costlier. Thus, for a seller, to make the customer's approved supplier list should be prized. However, poor or lazy buyers minimise their work by placing obstacles in the path of wannabe suppliers. Some large European firms do push it a little too far by demanding suppliers and even potential suppliers pay a €1,000 annual fee to get onto and remain on the 'permitted supplier list'. Others reduce their workload in vetting prospective suppliers by making it hard to get to see the buyer. Larger UK supermarkets have even been accused of charging suppliers 'slotting fees' or 'pay-to-stay fees', to effectively compel suppliers to rent shelf space in the supermarket. Such commercial practices are ethically dubious and potentially in breach of industry guidelines governing relationships with suppliers. Furthermore, they are potentially damaging to the quality of the 'approved suppliers list'. Large buyers can sometimes abuse their supplier base by over-excising their power by demanding unrealistic pricing and terms. In doing so, they render it uneconomic or unduly hard for small to medium sized enterprises (SMEs) to do business with them. As a consequence, the large buyer's supplier list gets smaller and now unsurprisingly consists of predominantly larger suppliers, and thereby the buyer's power has been self-eroded.

The approved supplier list should be a dynamic one, constantly updated and refreshed so the firm creates competition for its business, and thereby obtains the best value for money. Supplier auditing should not be a one-off affair but repeated periodically to ensure no deterioration in the supplier's condition and status. However, buyers who are lazy or are buried in the production department and locked in 'routine clerical processing' tend to neglect these 'network development and maintenance' aspects of their role. Under such conditions where the 'approved supplier list' becomes short, biased toward large firms and stagnant, the buyer creates the conditions conducive for its suppliers to collude and form an informal de-facto cartel, which will be to the detriment of the commercial viability of the firm.

Given my international experience and as a commercial director, I accompanied our purchasing manager to India to assess potential suppliers of raw materials and goods for resale. It was the manager's first such overseas trip. Previously, like many European companies in our industry, we had been buying raw materials via UK traders and agents of overseas manufacturers who had until then supplied most of our knowledge of our Indian suppliers. To say the trip was an eye-opener is an understatement.

Over the next two weeks we travelled up and down the country from Ahmedabad to Poona. We visited factories, sometimes uninvited, sometimes invited at short notice, peered over walls and generally asked a lot of sometimes not well-received questions. We found many good companies, whom utilising second-mover advantage had designed out the process and commercial problems that their European competitors lived with. Overall, they were at least as well-managed from an environmental and health and safety perspective. On the other hand, we found some factories that were little more than Dickensian hell-holes. Some factories we had been told were closed, as it turned out by a middleman with conflicts of interest, were in fact open. Some factories that supposedly existed actually didn't. They were no more than vacant building plots of some size, occupied by sparse vegetation and surrounded by high walls with an impressive gatehouse and a single site office building set within. Some factories we visited with the alleged owners turned out to be borrowed for the day, with a freshly painted sign outside. Many were no more than a telephone and fax number, yet their names were listed in significant industry market reports and trade directories. I wasn't entirely surprised. I'd had a similar experience in China, where many companies were no more than a website with a phone and fax line. Where India differed was the extent to which the middlemen would distort and try to cover up the reality of the situation. This went to the extent of multiple sourcing goods, repackaging them with the brand of a reputable company and then selling them on as 'bona fide' uniform single-sourced branded goods. If the lack of product quality and consistency proved a problem, the middleman would pretend to arrange an alternate source. In reality they just put the same mixed source product in the packages with the new 'alleged' pukka source's name on it. In the largest scale case of this fraud I encountered to get around the ISO requirements of the end user, the actual repackaging and fakery was done in the UK!

One of the worst examples I have encountered in my career was on that tour at the Vatva Industrial Estate in Ahmedabad. We were scheduled at short notice to visit the factory of a middle-ranking colorant maker who supplied many of the European majors in our market. I well recall the day was fine and not excessively hot. We had chosen our tour to follow shortly after the monsoon when the climate was more hospitable for Europeans, and India would be at its best, having been washed clean with a good flush of rain. We were driven from our hotel near the airport on the outskirts of town to the estate, passing as we went the rusting corrugated iron shanties that proliferate in and around most Indian cities. I recall chains of school children, a couple of dozen at a time, holding hands with one another, with one sari-clad teacher in the front leading the first child by the hand, and another at the back holding the hand of the last in the chain. I recall musing at the improvised 'school bus' and being amazed as the children wound out of their poor hovels in the shanty, how clean and smart they all looked, immaculately dressed in white shirts and blouses and smart pressed blue shorts and skirts, each having an old-fashioned polished leather satchel on their back. The value that Indians place on education and a desire to learn at every level in society is one that many Europeans would love to emulate with the children at a national level. And indeed, with education being the key to adult financial success, the practice is one that ethical companies should seek to encourage in developing countries. As we drove up for our appointment at the plant, we arrived outside a now familiar set-up of high walled facilities with a solid gate. The exception was that this site had an effective moat, a large open drain running in front of its walls, deep and wide enough for a now half-purple water buffalo to wallow in, just a few yards from the factory gate. The gate opened and we entered across the permanent concrete bridge on foot leaving our car and driver outside. The broadly smiling owners of the plant greeted us warmly and pointed out their waste treatment facilities by their gatehouse as we adjourned to a clean, tidy and air-conditioned meeting room in the site offices. We had the usual sales pitch from the firm on how great their product was performing in most applications to the highest specification, and how it complied with all the regulatory requirements for EN European safety standards, and how ecologically sound their process of manufacture was. At this point I requested to view their manufacturing buildings. The puzzled owners looked at one another with some concern, but as they'd painted themselves into a corner, they couldn't very well say no. Usually their visitors were commercial contacts and traders of products, who generally weren't technically orientated and couldn't tell a reactor vessel from a holding tank. They eventually consented and we got a tour of the site. The factory had all the basic plant to make the goods in question and had a significant capacity, although at the volumes this particular unit was manufacturing, it didn't have the capacity to make the quality of goods they claimed they sold. But the thing the plant didn't have were the necessities of a safety infrastructure – not even hand rails or indeed many walls to the elevated reactor floors. The walls had been omitted from the building to vent toxic fumes from the process with no extractor or scrubber to be found. Aside from the offices and driveway visible from the gate when opened, the plant, though clearly not old, was dirty, ramshackle, more reminiscent of a war zone than a factory and of course it was a health and safety nightmare. In the place where you'd expect the most grime, where the product discharged from large filter presses into skips to be manually taken to the dryers, I found a number of children working with about three or four adults who looked more like casual field labourers than factory workers. I know the average Indian is somewhat smaller than a European, but even so, I judged the children's ages to be between 10 and 12 years old at most,[34] and no protective clothing in sight, not even for the adults. The children were discharging and cleaning down a framed chemical filter press. With full frames weighing upward of 70 kg, if cleaned manually in the UK, it would be the sort of job given to a pair of appropriately clad 16-stone rugby playing bruisers. In India, beneath the press was a skip and when the odd lump of product missed the skip and hit the floor, the children's mother was there sweeping up below with a handful of broom twigs. The reclaimed spilt product, its now associated dirt and broom twigs with it were being put into the product skip. That same product would carry that dirt into its next application as a finished good in Europe or the US. It was then that I said something tactless. *"Should those children be working in here?"* I said in a calm, measured tone directing the question to one of the owners. As I did I glimpsed the plant's overseer out of the corner of my eye. He had understood what was said and its implication, as his demeanour immediately changed from its prior casual expression to one of thunder. The owner, however, was unperturbed and in a relaxed manner, smiling casually before replying, *"Today's a school holiday; the children are just in for the day helping their parents."* Judging the mood of the overseer, I said nothing further on the issue and we progressed on our tour, following as I did the flow of materials and processes in the plant, the solid process waste we had witnessed being put in with the finished goods. The liquid process waste ran into an open gutter, thence into a four-inch pipe at ground level and from there in went through a rough hole punched in the factory wall near to the gate, with its outlet draining into the buffalo's bathing water. Ultimately all the outflow from the estate's open drain system ended up in a river four to five metres across, which ran faster than a good walking pace and was black with multiple chemical effluents, through the industrial estate. Of course, the 'alleged' water treatment plant was just a mock-up with a large tank of clean water and a sprinkler to give the impression (to the ill-educated) that the site had waste water treatment capabilities. On saying our cordial farewells at the gate and returning to our car, already knowing the answer, I asked our driver if the schools were on holiday. He responded smiling with a characteristically Indian wobble of the head, "*Sir, all the children that go to school are in school.*"

In my subsequent enquiries, I learned that the company was bussing in its casual labour from an agricultural area quite some distance from the city. The minibuses employed had blacked out windows so the locals could not see who came and went. They did this to avoid upsetting the local population as the gangmaster for the bussed labour, i.e. the overseer I met, only charged the equivalent of 70 cents per day for a man equivalent (i.e. two boys) compared with the local going union rate for casual labour which was a full dollar or slightly above for really dirty work. Needless to say, the gangmaster's clients didn't receive 70 cents but more likely half that. But that wasn't the sickest thing I learned about that company. They had several plants in the region, were of significant size, turning over many tens of millions of dollars, and their biggest stakeholder, in the form of a 60% debenture holding, was the Hong Kong subsidiary of a large British merchant bank. I later learned through a major German client that he had conducted a snap inspection of another factory in the Surat area belonging to the same firm and also found children working. To his credit, he struck the firm from his company's approved suppliers list.

5.2.2 Corrupt Buyers

On rare occasions, a buyer will go rogue. By this I mean the buyer will act in malfeasance, by accepting money or other rewards for favouring one particular seller over others, and rather than the buyer being corrupted by an unscrupulous seller, the buyer will be the instigator to the malfeasance. When this occurs, the relationship between buyer and sell is instantly transformed from symbiotic to parasitic, with the creation of an economically unstable illegitimate monopoly. In this case, it is the buyer who is the parasite. The rogue buyer keeps all other offers at bay, and the seller obviously has increased costs to bear in funding the buyer's reward. Thus, the good or service supplied to the organisation rises in price, perhaps even to the tune of 50% over the going market price for a commodity good or service. For the above conditions to arise and thrive, a least one or both of the following motivational elements is usually present:

(a) **High-P Buying Manager**: Poor appointments made in organisations under change conditions, i.e. expediency driven. High-P individuals are generally not suited to the detailed and systematised due diligence aspects of the buyer's role. However, driven by greed they may seek control over purchasing to milk a potentially lucrative situation.

(b) **Buying Manager's Broken Bond**: There is a breach in the psychological bond between the buyer and the firm. Probable causes are career frustration or perceived poor pay relative to their value to the firm, leading to a sense of grievance.

With the following situational conditions:

(1) **Sole control of the purchasing decision**: Many companies with turnovers under £25 million will employ a single buying manager with responsibility for purchasing up to £15 million in goods and services.

71

(2) **Ability to conceal**: Locating the purchasing manager in operations can place them in an environment where their co-workers have no frame of reference as to what is a good or bad price.

(3) **Lack of oversight**: Physically locating of the buyer distant from his line manager coupled with poor reporting. Lack of external market benchmarking of raw material/supply prices by unsophisticated boards.

(4) **Zero or low buyer rotation**: Buying manager is retained in post for a significant period of time where a dysfunctional system exists and the buyer is empowered to select his replacement; the dysfunctional behaviour may even be inherited by or sold on to the new incumbent of the post.

(5) **A corrupt seller**: A supplier is active in the market with the motive, means and capacity to meet the corrupt buying manager's demands.

The seller's premium can make the illegitimate monopoly visible or rapidly cause the demise of the firm. Thus, when you lift the lid off the situation where you have a clever corrupt buyer in the driving seat, as opposed to one who's just responding to a corrupt inducement from a seller, you tend to find that the buyer specifically targets key items on which he will misdeal. These are usually just one or two items or categories of items which probably make up less than 5% of products or services purchased, but could be 50% or more of the purchasing portfolio by value. The miscreant's aims being to make the scale of the reward worthwhile, less complex to transact and obscure and lower visibility to the host organisation. The corrupt buyer may even convince himself he's doing no harm, but the reality is such activities are an existential threat to the organisation. In the worst cases I've come across, the firms were closed or sold at a fraction of what should have been their worth to a market competitor who then instigated a turnaround where the buyer did not survive in the new entity. In one instance the same individual was likely the cause of both of the aforementioned, in one company after another. In the most brazen case I have ever come across, the buyer had actually set up a shell company which he controlled as a shadow director comprising a small warehousing unit on a trading estate manned by a single person. The buyer redirected the purchasing of the firm that employed him through his own shell company, and in doing so made handsome profits through overcharging his employer.

Quite clearly the above scenarios can only really be prevented by transparency, good reporting, compliance auditing and oversight. Structurally, placing the buyer within the commercial department aids transparency and oversight. It is also worth noting that in those nations, such as the German-speaking areas of Europe, where bribery payments were or are still tax-deductible, larger firms have a habit of routinely rotating buyers to very different operating divisions, such that the personal buyer-supply connections are routinely broken, or they will rotate the buyers with sales marketing staff within the wider commercial team. Thus, in major continental firms, it's less likely you'll find a buyer in the same post or managing the same purchasing portfolio for more than three years. Additionally, to facilitate transparency, where a single purchased key item accounts for €1 million per annum or more, the sourcing and purchasing decision is managed by at least two people in the organisation. Within larger organisations with multiple divisions, the parent organisation will typically collate all purchase pricing and quotations, with the compiled results being circulated to the purchasing managers and boards of its subsidiaries. Another positive feature of buying as a profession in continental Europe is that its value to the corporation is frequently rewarded with the respected title of 'prokurist'. In German-speaking regions only, prokurists are authorised officers of the firm responsible for negotiating for and on behalf of the organisation.

6. Theft and Fraud

6.1 Theft

Theft is an act where a person or persons dishonestly appropriate property belonging to another with the intention to permanently deprive the other. In most people's minds it conjures up images of mugging, pick-pocketing or burglary, but in business and commerce it can be a significant issue. Globally, billions of dollars of assets are physically stolen from businesses annually. In the developed West, hard asset thefts by organised gangs plague whole sectors of agriculture, construction, haulage and shipping. The United Nations Conference on Trade and Development (UNCTAD) estimated piracy costs ranged from US$1 billion, up to US$16 billion in 2014.[35] It is no longer an exception to lose a ship as large as a super tanker; such events now happen on a regular basis in waters of the Far East to East Africa. In the UK alone, theft of heavy plant and equipment from the construction industry amounted to an estimated staggering £800 million in 2015 with theft from farms adding circa £45 million. However you stack it, if your business has an asset that isn't nailed down and conveniently has wheels or can float, there's someone out there who'll be only too happy to permanently deprive you of it. And even if it is nailed down that won't prevent theft. With ferrous and nonferrous metals prices reaching new highs, metal thefts are reaching new extremes. It doesn't matter if it's the lead on the roof or even antique bells; churches and even cathedrals have been raided from Europe to North America. Copper cabling from railways has been stolen in UK, France and the Netherlands, even while they were still carrying live current. War memorials and works of art are not exempt. In the UK, a large Henry Moore bronze reclining female figure weighing two tonnes and valued at up to £3 million on the art market was stolen and sold to be melted down for scrap for just £1,500. War memorial plaques are routinely stolen and even the commemorative plaques from the

75

former Theresienstadt concentration camp in the Czech Republic were stolen. There is quite literally no item of any material worth that left unguarded will not attract thieves. It doesn't matter what its cultural value is or how sacred the object.

The implications for business are clear – all substantive assets must be physically protected and where business-critical properly insured. In designing premises, businesses will routinely take into consideration health and safety matters, but beyond locking doors and windows at night and turning on the burglar alarms, do we ever really consider asset security? The finance director will instinctively lock away the petty cash, but who would think to ensure that the forklift trucks in the warehouse should be chained to the building and have vehicle immobilisers fitted to ensure they are not taken? Agriculture and construction are particularly vulnerable and fitment of GPS tracking and vehicle immobilisers is now almost standard on new purchases. You wouldn't think you could lose a ship to piracy and not find it again, but it does happen. In such circumstances shipping lines need to consider covert GPS monitoring that not even the crew can disable. From a design standpoint, companies need to design out theft risk to minimise the merchantability of stolen goods. For example, railway signalling cable once copper, in some areas has been replaced with aluminium, as it is lower in cost per comparative length, and even metal cabling is now being replaced with fibre-optic lines, for which there is negligible black-market resale value.

6.2 Cybercrime

Regardless of what business does, theft will always be present, with the nature of what is stolen and how it's stolen constantly evolving over time. In today's internet interlinked world, theft has changed. You can be robbed without leaving your home and without the perpetrator physically entering it. Now it's cybertheft, and the cyberthief is after your identity, your data and your company's secrets. Hitting as many as one in ten people and two thirds of businesses, cyber criminals target individuals primarily seeking access to bank accounts and cards. MacAfee in 2014 estimated costs of cybercrime worldwide to be US$445 billion[36] and a recent study by Jupiter Research in 2016 estimated costs are likely to rise as high as US$2.1 trillion by 2019.

To quote Jim Gee, partner and head of Forensic and Counter Fraud Services PKF Littlejohn LLP, *"Unless you know the nature and scale of fraud, how can you implement an effective solution?"* Fraud at its simplest is a wrongful or criminal deception intended to result in financial or personal gain for the perpetrator at the expense of the victim. Fraud in the UK alone in all its manifestations including cybercrime, costs an estimated £193 billion with the private sector accounting for £144 billion, that directed toward people £10 billion, and the public-sector fraud £37.5 billion.[37] To put things in perspective, a super tanker loaded with crude oil and spirited away by pirates would set back its insurers a mere £250 million at today's prices. Governments concern themselves greatly with issues of cyberattacks, cyberterrorism, cyberwarfare, etc., but the element of cybercrime of concern to business and the individual and with greatest economic impact is financial-related fraud, principally through phishing, hacking and data theft. The size and scope of the implications of theft, fraud and in particular cybercrime, in the commercial world means it has to be brought into our strategic business decision-making.

We live in a computer-driven world but consider this: do we really need to put everything on computer and online? If it's not online, it can't be hacked. Therefore, the first line of defence must be to only put online what is necessary, and where this is financially sensitive, restrict access as far as possible. Where data is stored must be secure, especially where that security is entrusted into the hands of a third party. Where we have constructed a 'cyber citadel' in our corporation free of spyware and protected by the best firewall we can afford, it has to stay that way. That means no other device – stick or even mobile phone – must be allowed to connect to our clean system. It is not unheard of for promotional giveaway memory sticks from China to be found with spyware on them. Once connected to your system, you've inadvertently let in an e-burglar and invited them to hack your company's confidential and commercially sensitive data. Today, all our personnel have to be tech savvy and technical discipline enforced rigidly. I would also suggest against entrusting sensitive identity and finance data storage in newly developing nations that have a poor track record on issues relating to confidentiality. To me, this is just asking for trouble. I have seen several examples where manpower cost considerations have prompted corporations to base computer data keying processing and call centres overseas, and in doing so, they have compromised data security, thus necessitating further expense to rectify the matter. Data breaches in India are a particular risk.[38]

6.3 Internal Fraud

With new methods of theft and fraud in management's focus, we shouldn't forget good old-fashioned fraud. As starkly stated by Bucy et al, the primary reason that people steal is *"because they can"*. From an understanding of the mechanics of how and why fraud occurs (Figure 3) we have a chance to address the challenges of prevention and detection. Its *prima facia* cause being financial need or greed, but the real cause lies in its motivational factors in the snake pit, which we have discussed earlier.

Figure 3 – The Mechanics of Fraud in the Corporate Environment

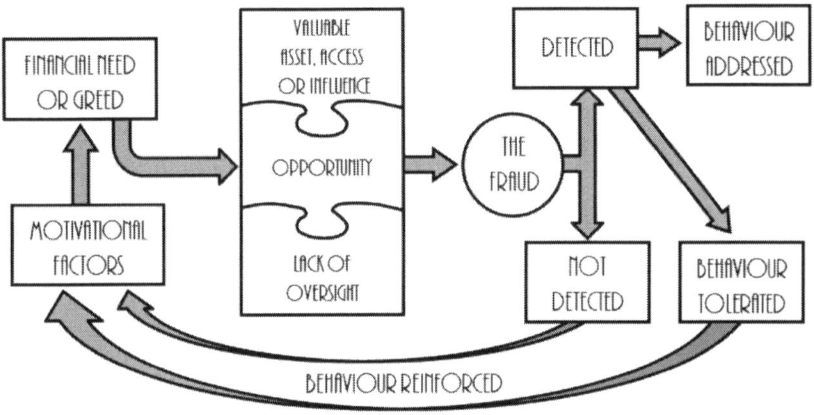

Fire requires a combination of factors: source of heat, fuel and oxygen. In the case of fraud, our source of heat is *motivation*. Access to valuable assets worth stealing or influence worth selling provides the incentive or fuel, and lack or supervision provides the oxygen that can magnify the tendency to crime. Given this unholy triad, if opportunity is not already present, the motivated miscreant will create it. Failure to address a fire leads to it spreading. It's the same with fraud. If not checked, the success of the stratagem will only serve to reinforce motivation to repeat the same, and thereby the dysfunctionality perpetuates in a vicious cycle.

Most incidents of theft and fraud from firms, with perhaps the exception of cybercrime, are inside jobs. Naturally those with most access to valuable assets and their manipulation have the most opportunity, and it's probably true that there are more accountants and bookkeepers in jail per capita than any other profession, and more crime by value committed by financial advisers and bankers. For example, the Bernie Madoff Ponzi scheme was estimated to be a US$64.8 billion fraud. If you were to stack end to end the number of petty criminals who'd collectively stolen as much, they'd stretch from the earth to the moon.

Magicians are the ultimate deceivers. Through their tricks with smoke and mirrors or sleight of hand coupled with distraction, they can even make an elephant seemingly disappear on stage. And it is the same with criminal fraud. When perpetrated, the fraudster seeks to deceive by hiding their actions whilst management's attention is otherwise distracted from where it should be focussed, or by creating a barrier of deceit to obscure the fraud. If the fraudster is any good, how can you spot them let alone guard against such individuals? There is an old saying 'Fog is the Fraudster's Friend'. Look for the distraction and the fog, and where you find that, there is the possibility of fraud. For example, in a case I had a hand in uncovering, the QuickBooks computer system the company was employing was in utter chaos and management reports from it were almost useless. Seeing the fog, the group finance director did the only thing he could do, he brought in a new bookkeeper, one with banking experience at a senior level with a cognisance of fraud and a nitpicking eye for detail. The old bookkeeper had, as it turned out, been misdirecting commissions and some of the firm's commerce through his own company. In another case I came across, the miscreant relied on the distraction of a thinly stretched management team during a succession crisis. In an ill-perceived fraud, he destroyed properly authorised cheques made out to suppliers, and reissued cheques with forged signatures in the same amount to himself. The management didn't discover the cumulative fraud until the disgruntled suppliers who hadn't received payment finally became such an issue that they bypassed the purchase ledger clerk to complain.

The simple remedy to prevent fraud is transparency and discipline in operational and financial recordkeeping and money management with oversight. Ideally all payments should be made by direct transfer, thereby creating an irrefutable and auditable paper trail. Payments of large sums, size dependent upon your organisation, should be dually authorised by appropriate directors. Such systems need to be robust and crisis resistant, so that if a director is unexpectedly drawn away from the business, a deputy or prokurist stands in. Those that keep the records shouldn't be those that authorise payment or issue cheques. Get it wrong and a lot of money can vanish very quickly. Above all watch out for '*fog*'; it's the sure sign of increased financial risk.[39]

6.4 Fraud in Commerce

Fraud in commerce is a comparatively uncomplicated and straightforward (or should that be crooked) matter of corruption of the transaction between buyer and seller. Here the perpetrator seeks to pass off goods to which he has either no title to, thus can't legally sell, or misdescribes goods of lesser worth, or no worth, passing them on as something they are not. Counterfeit goods, such as Rolex copy-watches are classic examples of a sales fraud – when sold purporting to be the real thing. But such frauds are not restricted to faked branded goods, which are awash the world over. Prior frauds have included fake baby milk (in reality hazardous melamine dispersion), rice (made of plastic, it being cheaper than real rice), textile dyes (impure chemicals made from industrial waste), fake pigments, fake vodka (really industrial methylated spirits or pure industrial alcohol), fake cigarettes and other tobacco products (made with tobacco of dubious origin), fake food dyes (in reality, cheaper leather dyes deem toxic for human consumption), fake spices (e.g. cinnamon, which is in reality wood dust with a sprinkling of synthetic cinnamon flavouring), fake aircraft spares (from scrapped aircraft, passed off as new), fake antiques (an ancient trade going back many hundreds of years), fake insurance (it's really very cheap, just don't try to claim), fake gold bars (real gold bars purporting to be issued by Fort Knox but hollowed out and packed with cheaper tungsten powder filling), even fake business ventures (e.g., Nigerian 419 frauds, Nasdaq 'pump-and-dump' scams). There's almost nothing that can't be faked and used to commit fraud. To add to the fakes, there's a thriving world market in stolen goods purporting to be legitimate.

When it comes to the fraudsters' cons, consumers generally have protection of nationally applicable consumer goods laws. These are generally 'non-contract out-able of' and at least afford a method of retaliation in law, and a route to recompense. For the businessman, it's not quite so simple. Proving the other party set out to mislead and misrepresent what was transacted, and that it formed part of the contract, can be quite an issue. It's all down to the clarity of the contract and what is provable. For the most part that's what is specifically; what's committed to paper, and most contracts will contain a *'whole agreement'* clause defining the limitations of the agreement, for example:

> *"This agreement, and any documents referred to in it, constitute the whole agreement between the parties and supersede all previous arrangements, understandings and agreements between them, whether oral or written, relating to their subject matter.*

Each party acknowledges that in entering into this agreement, and any documents referred to in it, it does not rely on, and shall have no remedy in respect of, any representation or warranty (whether made innocently or negligently) that is not set out in this agreement or those documents."

6.5 Who's Conning Whom?

Consider this scenario: A chemicals industry executive working in mergers and acquisitions wishes to acquire new processes to enhance his company's product portfolio. He is approached by a smaller firm producing a food dye product and it's just the type of value-added niche product process the executive is seeking. Under a confidentiality agreement, the executive agrees to review the process to evaluate its viability. He receives a package of documents including the detailed process recipe, raw material and product's food-grade specifications. He later visits the production site. All he is being offered and proposes to buy is the recipe – not the plant and not the small firm. Like all people conducting due diligence, he has his eyes open and is taking in all that is shown to him – and also things that are not. He has discussions in the small firm's site office about how the workers are organised to man the process. In doing so, he cannot escape his eye being caught by a graph, prominently placed on the wall behind the desk of the small business owner. This apparently is displaying an improving yield over time for the process on offer. The documentation he has been given for the yield of the process on offer is 65%. The graph on the wall implies the reality is that over time, the yield has been improved to 85% (which he assumes by learning curve experience). The graph is not discussed, noted or pointed out by the seller. The executive calculates that at a 65% yield, the process is not worth buying at the price the seller is asking but at 85% yield and the same raw material cost base, it's very much worth buying. The executive does not discuss the yield discrepancy with the seller for fear he will drive up the asking price. He subsequently buys the process, thinking he's got a good deal.

Back in his own company the executive handed the process to his research and development team. They seemingly can't make the process work or at least to work well; the yield was at best 65%. The lead chemist points out that if you up the yield beyond 65%, the quality of the product would drop radically and it couldn't then be sold as food quality. The only other application for off-specification dye of that type was small, being limited to pet food applications and prices there were very poor for such low-grade materials. On further investigation, the seller turned out to be a serial seller of processes and was litigious. He could not compete in the food-grade dye market with his process and his only outlet for his product was small in scale and into the pet food trade.

Who conned whom: did the cunning seller con the executive by hiding behind contract law, or did the executive con himself through his own naivety and greed? Or perhaps both were parties to a con?

6.6 Long Fraud and the Role of Shadow Directors

Traditional *'long firm fraud'* otherwise known as *'consumer credit fraud'* is a fraud that utilises a limited liability trading company for fraudulent purposes. The basic operation is to run the company as an apparently 'legitimate' business by buying goods and paying suppliers promptly to secure a good credit record. The fraudsters then commence to stretch their credit as far as possible. Once they are sufficiently well-established, the perpetrators then purchase the next round of goods on credit and then disappear with both the goods and profits from previous sales. The goods are then sold off elsewhere, the suppliers are left as out-of-pocket victims and are nonplussed as to what they did wrong.

Long firm frauds, once popular in the mid-20th century, have become significantly less common in recent years since it is no longer possible to operate for any length of time without leaving a significant identity and banking paper trail. This makes it almost impossible for the perpetrators to get away with the cash by simply disappearing behind a new identity. However, modern variants of long firm fraud do exist. Instead of disappearing, the perpetrators play a longer game by bleeding cash from the firm. This thereby renders the firm technically bankrupt with intent to avoid liability to their debtors in the form of their suppliers, lenders, HMRC, their employee's pension funds and even other stockholders in the enterprise through abuse of insolvency rules and their limited liability status. Whilst I have witnessed such events on a small scale, the reader would do well to consider that they also occur on a grand scale and for a general education in the subject it is well worth studying the career and frauds of the late Robert Maxwell.

As if to add insult to injury, in some cases, within days, the perpetrators of long frauds buy the bankrupt firm's assets and its now devalued stock back from the court-appointed receiver and commence trading the same goods from the same premises but under a different company name. In such cases the creditors of the bankrupt firm might receive back as little as 5 or 10 pence in the pound owed, and the perpetrators get away with the true realisable value of cash and goods lost by the creditors. After all, running a company into the ground by incompetent management is not a crime, and proving the intent to defraud creditors would be problematic.

How can such situations arise? Well, usually the perpetrator acts as a 'shadow director' or 'de-facto' director in real control of the company and hides behind a nominee or series of nominee directors whose names are publicly registered at Companies House in his stead. Moreover, the fiscal stain of bankruptcy usually does not attach itself to the perpetrators, particularly if they run their company as a *'shadow director'*. Instead the onus is carried by the dissolved firm or the individual who acts as a nominee director for the shadow director. If anyone gets disqualified as a director, it will be the nominee who will take the fall.

How can you avoid getting caught in such a trap? From a higher-level perspective, for UK companies it is possible to obtain public Companies House filings and accounts. Some accounting firms such as Merlin Scott Associates[40] will provide these compiled by industry sector, over a period of several years. A rapid analysis of a potential customer's trading performance can be obtained from an assessment of their net worth. Over and above using the industry norm as a benchmark, expressing their stock, debtors and creditors as ratios in relation to sales days, along with the trend of the figures gives a much more informed view to the ongoing viability of any particular account. Other credit websites offer simplistic credit reference scores for those seeking a fast but rough guide. I would caution against reliance on such credit assessments as they are often far too simplistic. They might inform you if a company has a County Court Judgement (CCJ) against them but they won't inform you of the reason why. This might range from alarming to trivial and they won't warn you of the risks posed by the presence of a shadow director.

Usually in a situation where the perpetrators have found a successful recipe to make money, they repeat the behaviour. Thus, owner managers of multiple bankruptcies, though not legally serial bankrupts in their own person, should be best avoided but in extremis, if pushed to do business with them, dealt with purely on a 'cash with order' basis. You can also ensure that your terms of doing business are on your Conditions of Sales, ensuring that ownership of any goods does not transfer to the customer 'until paid for in full'. This will at least give you a chance to wrest back your unused goods from the receiver if you act promptly.

An experienced sales manager will regularly visit his customers, and in doing so will pick up incidental gossip and get a feel for the customer's operations and workplace culture. That manager, as an experienced industry practitioner, should be on the lookout for malignancies diagnostic of a troubled enterprise, and be able to make a structured assessment as to the commercial viability of the customer's business and by inference his creditworthiness far better than any bank and way better than a credit reference website.

Most markets, even international markets, are comparatively small, and individuals can gain reputations that span continents. To spot individuals of dubious reputation, there is no substitute for longstanding market knowledge, of the type usually carried by the oldest and most beer-soaked member of the would-be supplier's sales team. Such individuals might not have the best sales figures but at times they can save you from being fleeced by many times their own salary. I am thankful for such individuals in my career as on one occasion, an old hand pointed out to me that an individual requesting credit terms had been behind three bankruptcies within a ten-year period, taking his creditors for up to £500,000 per bankruptcy and then each time buying back his company's assets from the same receiver for a minute fraction of the liabilities of his old trading company.

In particular, the sales manager will usually pick up who is the real boss and in a situation where this differs from who's recorded as a director on the companies register you likely have a 'shadow director'. Why is this a problem, as the reality is that a shadow director, if proven to be such, has exactly the same legal liabilities as a registered company director? The crux of the issue is 'if proven to be such'. If a controlling person or de-factor director in the company seeks to disguise the fact by not being registered as a director, then it is quite probable that that person is seeking to avoid his or her legal liabilities, and likely be doing this for nefarious reasons. Chief amongst those reasons will likely be seeking to avoid being disqualified as a company director and legally sanctioned via the criminal courts or civil litigation, should the enterprise hit the rocks. Put simply, shadow directorship within a limited liability corporation is a long-fraudsters safety net. They may also be acting as a shadow director by virtue of necessity, owing to having been previously struck off as a director. An additional complication would be that a shadow director will likely be excluded from the company's directors' insurance. That's assuming the company has valid insurance in the first place.

A person is not a shadow director if they are simply offering advice to a board and the board are acting on that advice. In general, a person is a shadow director if they are directly in a business-controlling position. Tell-tale signs might include:

- Taking the de-facto lead role or leading role in the company's governing structure.

- Controlling the company's financial affairs.

- Acting as sole signatory for the company bank account.

- Negotiating with third parties on behalf of the (nominal) board.

- Recruiting and appointing senior managers, and terminating the same.

The real giveaway will be who's at the top of the pecking order, occupying the symbolic throne in the organisation, i.e. the guy in the big chair in the largest corner office will be the de-facto boss no matter what his title, and if he's not a registered director then there's a problem.

As a point of note, the number of rogue directors struck off by the UK Government's Insolvency Service for criminal activity rose by almost a half during 2014/2015. The most common reasons for being struck off are false accounting and fraud. In the UK, a developed nation with generally good governance and a well-regulated business sector comprising less than 1% of the world's population and circa 3.9% of global GDP, 119 directors were struck off in UK tax year 2014/2015, compared to just 65 during the previous period. However, I think we can take it that there are many times that number of rogue directors walking the streets than the system has identified, and globally in less well-regulated nations the numbers are far higher. This increase comes despite the fact that Her Majesty's Insolvency Service has shrunk by 21% since 2007. It should be said that in the past the Insolvency Service was slow to take action against rogue directors, but in the last few years it appears to be sharpening up its act.

If you detect a situation where you suspect a company is being run by a shadow director, my recommendation is that you stay well clear. It's a critical indicator of the poor ethical health of a company and by inference there is higher commercial risk of doing business with it.

The strategic implications should be self-evident for any sales-based organisation not just those who are SMEs. Your outward-facing commercial personnel need to be alert and savvy in assessing their clients, and not just a bunch of order takers chasing this month's sales target. Alas today, too much sales training revolves around getting the order, which is frequently misnamed *'closing the sale'*. It's essential to have a team smart enough to spot commercial opportunities and gain orders. However, at the risk of stating the obvious, the term *'sale'* is defined as the exchange of a good or service for money, and usually involves getting the order, fulfilling it to an agreed specification in a timely manner and, above all, getting paid promptly. So, it's equally essential to have a properly commercially trained sales team, who can spot threats to the latter. And it's equally important to have commercial leadership with the courage and convictions in their abilities to be able to body swerve what on the face if it might be an attractive commercial proposition but in reality is one that carries major financial risk. You might feel that you miss some commercial opportunities not doing business with that iffy company, but you and your finance director will sleep easier.

7. The Contract Minefield

Given that the law of contract is the cornerstone of business dealing and has existed since the foundation of human society, it is too complex and immense a subject to cover in this text in anywhere close to its entirety. What I shall attempt to do is sketch out the basic elements of contract as broadly experienced in business and point to some of the unexploded mines that the business practitioner would do well to avoid stepping on. Ultimately it is hoped that such information will lead the practitioner to formulate better and more lasting contractual relations.

7.1 Contract in a Nutshell

What is contract? To most practitioners of law it's the formation of an agreement, whether written or verbal, that is legally binding on the parties freely entering into it. Through necessity the vast majority of contracts are committed to writing. There are many types of contract and many forms of commercial communication that can collectively form commercial contract on supply of goods or services, in addition to formal quotes, specifications and terms of sale or purchase. However, the key components of a typical formal business contract broadly encompass the following:

- The identities of the parties agreeing to the contract.

- The statement acknowledging the parties to the contract wish to be bound by law.

- The nature of the contract, whether it's an agreement to sell, license, lease, rent, agency, etc. or simply a memorandum of understanding.

- What is offered by whom, to whom, and for what value or consideration it is granted – the promises made and agreed to (i.e. the 'meeting of minds') between the parties and by which they agree to be legally bound.

- The terms and conditions of performance of the agreed promises between the parties.

- The time, event or date of the fulfilment of the promises made.

- As so many agreements are international and legal codes differ from jurisdiction to jurisdiction, the Jurisdiction and Governing Law under which agreement is formed is defined.

- The process by which any disputes are resolved.

- The formal physical proof of the 'meeting of minds' on the agreement i.e. the duly witnessed signatures of the parties authorised to make the agreement.

Contracts for illegal purposes are not legally   enforceable.   Also contracts to indemnify a person for the consequences of their engaging in an illegal act are also unenforceable (i.e. you can insure against the consequences of a crime happening to you but cannot get insurance for the consequences of you wilfully committing a crime). Notwithstanding the aforementioned, in most jurisdictions such illegal contracts if formulated could be construed as criminal conspiracy. And at this point I shouldn't have to say, don't do either, but I will. Absolutely do not contract into a criminal event, unless of course you are a career criminal and prepared to do the time if you're caught.

Thus far, Contract doesn't seem a daunting subject and most persons of average intellect, with a few examples of prior contracts could put together a good stab at a draft business agreement. However, Contract is not just about legal documents; it's far more than that in much the same way that marriage is far more than the marriage license and the legal statues that pertain to the marriage rights and in some cases divorce. When contracts are negotiated, the parties put each other on notice of the types of behaviour they expect of one another in addition to defining their rights and duties to one another. As such the contract process defines and establishes the culture and way the parties will do business and otherwise interact going forward. Thus the contract and its negotiation process is a behavioural management tool and not just a legal safety net documenting obligations and rights to be haggled over should the relationship fail.

7.2 Acting in Good Faith or Not?

The prerequisite for successful negotiation and contract is that all parties act in good faith. Acting in good faith in legal terms is what it says on the tin and understood by common parlance; acting with honesty and the sincere intent to deal fairly with others, without malice or the desire to defraud. But here's the problem with 'good faith' and one that I did not know of despite my formal business education. To my chagrin I had to learn from another party's attorney. When in a dispute he declared that his client was under no obligation to negotiate in, or indeed, to act in 'good faith'. To me and those around me, the concept that someone would purposely set out to negotiate and deal in bad faith was utterly alien. How could there be any true 'meeting of minds' with the other party having a hidden nefarious intent? Needless to say, I was stunned. I could hear my mother's words ringing in my ears, like a gypsy's warning, *"We're not business people"*. Luckily, and with a lot of help from my friends, I survived that dark episode, but many would-be entrepreneurs don't.

The key problem is that, unlike many other legal systems around the world, English common law and US Federal law do not recognise a general contractual duty to act in good faith either when negotiating or when performing contracts. There are some exceptions in English law, but these are not based on statute but based on legal precedent or 'judge-made law', notably by certain rulings by the late Lord Scarman, Master of the Rolls. Over recent years there have been a series of High Court cases which have tested this position and have shown an increasing willingness of the courts to imply good faith obligations in the performance of contracts, at least for long-term 'relational contracts' such as matters relating to intellectual property licensing, joint ventures, franchise and distribution arrangements. However, the traditional English law aversion to a general duty of good faith has so far survived these challenges.

The strategic consequences are clear. When drafting any contract, irrespective of national jurisdiction, it is essential to include a clause obligating all parties to negotiate and act in good faith in all matters relating to the performance of the contract and even in matters that survive that contract, such as residual obligations of commercial confidentiality. This will create a fiduciary duty between the parties obligating them to fair and honest dealings with each other. If you're not prepared to accept such terms, then you can abandon any pretence that you're an ethical business person. If the other party isn't prepared to accept such terms, politely say farewell, shake their hand, and walk out of the room, remembering to count your fingers on the way out. Some people are averse to contracting 'good faith' purely because, it establishes a 'legally enforceable' fiduciary duty between the parties.

For example, two parties, licensor and licensee, have agreed an exclusive licensing agreement for a technology distribution, and the licensee subsequently decides that they want to commercialise a competing technology they've subsequently developed. The licensee is now caught in a conflict of interest, and may consider 'license squatting', i.e. using the already contracted rights of exclusivity, but not performing the duties envisaged at the license's formation, to effectively exclude the licensor's product from the market. This would kill off some of the licensee's potential competition for his new process. Had the parties contracted in good faith, there would be grounds that such an action would constitute a breach of the fiduciary duty of the licensee to the licensor, and hence grounds for termination of the contract with the possibility of damages payable to the licensor.

Where there is no contracted good faith, the licensor is on uncertain ground and depending on which jurisdiction the contract falls under, could be potentially barred from the market for the term of the non-performing license. The last line of defence of the licensor would be to fall back on any presumed 'good faith' provision in civil codes or 'legal precedent' and trust that certain judge-made rulings in case law favouring presumption of good faith. Regardless of the presumption of good faith in law in any jurisdiction, to avoid doubt and to put all parties on notice what is expected of one another, always include a clause obligating good faith. Together with inclusion of performance criteria and terms for termination for non-performance, this is essential in the United States, as the use of 'license squatting' is a common commercial tactic to block potential competitors.

Aside from the issue of contract, it is essential that in your business dealings and negotiations you be 'streetwise'. That does not mean that you should not be trusting. After all, it's almost impossible to do business productively with someone you don't trust to a good degree, but someone intent on acting in bad faith is hardly likely to say at the outset: *"Hi I'm a crook and I'm going to do my best to rip you off."* To quote the late Ronald Reagan's quote to the Mikhail Gorbachev during the 1980s SALT talks, *Doveryai, no proveryai – "trust, but verify"*. For example, if you assign agency rights for a particular national market, you should still be able to enter that country to conduct market research as to the performance of the agent without them controlling what you do and who you see. Otherwise how else could you be able to objectively ascertain that agent's performance and verify their good faith?

When perpetrators of unethical or illegal conduct find a successful recipe to make money, they usually repeat that behaviour. This is usually visible to others and can create a market reputation which reveals a pattern of behaviour. I shouldn't have taken what I was told as gospel by the contracting parties that I had problems with. I should have spoken to third parties in the industry and checked on the background of their associates. Had I done my homework better, it would have exposed poor commercial reputation, prior litigious behaviour including shoddy legal practice, criminality and allegations of the same. Forewarned, I could've avoided expending a lot of blood and treasure. It should be needless to say, but here it is anyway: Avoid doing business with serial litigants especially those who engage in *vexatious litigation*'. Moreover, I recommend avoiding those who have attorneys who have a track record of being involved in the same. To know what's' happening in a market and about the individuals and companies acting within it, it pays to have a good network of contacts and friends. I cannot recommend highly enough the building and maintenance of a good supportive network of likeminded individuals. Above all, on your part always act in good faith and document your actions, as if and when 'the shit hits the fan' and your company or you end up in litigation, the rightness of your conduct and its provability will be your best defence.

7.3 The Small Print Means More Than It Says

Whilst an industry practitioner should be able to make a good stab at drafting commercial contract, I would never recommend using that draft live unless it had been vetted at least at some point by a legal professional and preferably a sector experienced lawyer. Some might think the legalese used in contracts just a matter of style and there's some truth in that, but in many critical instances specific words, nuance in the use of language and even punctuation really do matter. You'll typically find that, to avoid conflict in interpretation of legal meaning, especially in language translation, patent attorneys in particular will attempt to draft in as short a sentence as practical and avoid use of punctuation as far as possible.

Words are of critical importance. Let's take the specific example of *'will'* and *'shall'*. In today's common parlance, will and shall are used virtually interchangeably, both inferring certainty about a future event. And, to the 'nit-picking', in modern written British grammar, the rule is that will should only be used with second and third person pronouns (you; he, she, it, they). With first person pronouns (I and we), the 'correct' verb to talk about the future is *'shall'*. Yet in the US, given that many US citizens are not of British descent, and non-native British-English speakers from other European countries and Latin America, and in Latin-derived languages, there is no cognitive equivalent to 'shall', the US Government's own Plain Language group advocates not using the word 'shall' in modern US-English.

Irrespective of a person's education, whether from Eton, a British Comprehensive, Harvard or the Bronx, English law and by inference much of the law of Commonwealth countries and the United States, is heavily based on case law, which has built up over many hundreds of years. The words 'will' and 'shall' have historic different meanings being derived from Old English, *'willan'* meaning 'want' or 'wish' and *'sceal'* meaning 'obligation'. The current legal meanings of 'will' and 'shall' in Contract Law take their precedents from 18th and 19th century case-proven use of the words, wherein 'shall' specifically refers to obligation to perform the future event, whereas 'will' relates to a promissory action or a desire to perform that action, with the important difference in emphasis being – at personal volition of the party making that promise. Thus, the legal use of 'will' in Anglo-Saxon law jurisdictions does not carry the same mandatory obligation as 'shall' to perform a contracted action. Few speakers still make the distinction in usage or abuse of these words, but in legal terms the distinctive historic case-proven meanings are generally upheld.

The use of small print can convey more than just the meaning of individual words and clauses. Picture this scenario: You are negotiating a licensing agreement for intellectual property under a memorandum of understanding, permitting the other party a time-limited exclusivity period to negotiate a technology license. At some expense, your attorneys have just drafted an 18-page contract and you forward the draft to the potential licensee for discussion. The other party's attorney reviews it and adds their input to the document, but in doing so, at some 40+ instances in the document, in clauses relating to obligations and duties of the licensee to perform, deletes the word 'shall' and replaces it with 'will'. Yet at the same time including the word 'shall' in other obligations of the licensor to the licensee. You simply comment on the word change and ask why? The other party's representative, an experienced commercial director with a formal business education, who's negotiated many acquisitions and licensing agreements tells you *"it's just a stylistic and presentational matter"* and adds *"they mean the same thing anyway."* Do they mean the same thing, and do you want to take the chance? In some jurisdictions and cultures this is the normal general horse trading and rough and tumble of business negotiation, but in others the same actions would be deemed as deception, breach of 'good faith' and more than sufficient reason to walk away from negotiations. Either way, what picture does the scenario paint of the respect of the other party toward you? And what are the implications for your faith in the trustworthiness of the other party going forward?

7.4 Card Shark-canery

When I was fourteen years old, in secondary school and just before the commencement of an afternoon lesson, our French teacher, Mr Mullen caught myself and a group of friends playing cards for money. Instead of the expected exclamation of moral indignation followed by a lecture on our depravity, as we'd have received from many other members of staff, Mullen said, *"Deal me in lads."* Well, why not, we all thought – better than being sent to the Gaffer (our nickname for the headmaster, Mr Hutchison) for six of the best. And yes, they did beat you with a bamboo cane in those days – on the hands for minor infringements of discipline and on the behind for anything else. The Gaffer deemed it a nod of humanity on his part, as the deputy headmaster, being a Scot of belligerent nature, wanted to use the Tawse but was prevented from doing so. As was customary, the winner of the last hand dealt the cards, and it came to the occasion that Mullen won and was handed the deck. He dealt and we all played, but he kept on winning. Sensing the cards were seemingly falling very much in the teacher's favour one of our number commented on his remarkable skill at cards. Mullen said, *"Lads, since you've been such goods sports, I'll let you into my little secret. I've been dealing my hand from the bottom of the deck for the last half dozen games and none of you have noticed."* Then he added, *"If you can't spot when the dealer's a card shark, don't play for money."* With that a major life's lesson was learned … and the class had only just started.

A salutary lesson indeed and long remembered, but I never thought I'd need the same skills as a grown-up in a business environment. That was until the time I, as a young management executive, accompanied our company secretary to a management group meeting. I entered his room at the appointed time and he asked me to hold on while he finished the task at hand. He was just in the process of concluding a contract with a large client and was purposely reading and initialling every single page with a fountain pen before signing the contract on the last page, which I was then called on to witness. *"Why initial every page?"* I said, *"Don't you trust them?"* He replied, *"If I could trust them, do you think I'd need a contract in writing? The answer is, no I don't, and if they did try it on, it won't be the first deal where the other party has tried to swap a page and change agreed terms."* He then added, *"The last time it happened to me, the deed was done by the other party's lawyer, and I was in the room at the time."* Being a qualified lawyer himself and a good speed reader, he'd sensed something was amiss. Rereading the documents before they were signed, he found apparently two versions of the same contract in the room. Had the wrong version or both been signed, it could have been a career-ending mistake for him.

This example was not the last time that I've come across the issue of commercial conflicts caused by two differing versions of apparently the same signed contract. For the reader, I recommend you don't take the risk. Conveniently, e-mail with handy date-time stamping provides a good documentary paper trail, but page initialling and taking precautions against the other party for dealing off the bottom of the deck is a wise precaution on critical documents and a practice that has served me well in covering my backside over the years. As with all contracts, always ensure you are covered by a 'good faith' clause, as if the contracted relations end in arbitration or the courts, it could be all that saves you.

In the UK, lawyers take a professional oath and their first obligation is to the law, yet it's worth remembering lawyers aren't saints, and it's critical that you don't rely on the other party's lawyer/ attorney to be meticulous in their professional ethics. In England and Wales in 2015 over 120 lawyers were fined, suspended or struck off the professional register by the Solicitor's Disciplinary Tribunal for misconduct. In 2016, those figures exceeded 140 persons from January to October[41]. It's worth noting that in the US, an attorney's first obligation is to his client. So, overseas, be doubly on your guard, especially considering that in US, in 2011, nationally 1,046 attorneys were disbarred from practicing[42], and that ignores those who were merely fined. The figures indicate that in both the UK and US, annually roughly one lawyer/attorney out of every 1,000 practicing was proven to be involved in serious professional misconduct if not outright criminality. If you think that's disturbing, in 2012, the EU average was 12.5 pronouncements of reprimands, sanctions, or suspensions per 1,000 lawyers. To give some perspective with a stringently policed profession, in the UK, there are 0.3–0.4 doctors per 1,000 struck from the medical register annually.

7.5 Jurisdiction in International Commercial Law

7.5.1 The Global Legal Landscape

Essentially there are two dominant legal systems worldwide. England, the home of Anglo-Saxon common law, and the former dominions of the British Empire, including the Republic of Ireland, largely practice a common-law system where cases are primarily decided on the basis of legal precedent set in case law. The bulk of the rest of Europe, follow a code-law system, having its origins in old Roman law. As with the spread of English Common Law, the former dominions of the French and Spanish empires have inherited their Romanic code-law-based systems, as Civil Law. Due to accidents of history there are some anachronisms. For example, Scotland, Quebec, French Guyana and even the state of Mississippi practice a blend of code-based and common law. In countries practicing Romanic code law, the law and all its contingencies are laid out in a system of statutes and constitute the National Civil Code. The statutes are subject to commentary by the judicial administration but the commentaries are not precedents in the common law by which a judge can be bound, but merely serve to clarify the intentions of the original statutes as laid out by the legislature to form part of the Basic Law. The other key difference between the law code systems is that jury trials are unique to Anglo-Saxon common law whereas code-law adjudication is purely by bench trial (i.e. a judge or magistrate or a panel thereof).

The choice of jurisdiction on a particular contractual matter would on the face of it be obvious for any business practitioner, naturally favouring his own domestic civil law. After all, it's what he's familiar with, and as the saying goes; 'east, west, home is best'. However, as observed by Benvenisti and Downs[43] (respectively Professor of Law, Tel Aviv University and Professor of Politics, New York University), in their discourse on the role of national courts, domestic democracy and the evolution of International Law:

> *"National courts have their own characteristic weaknesses as well as strengths. Ultimately they remain agents of their states, and more often than not reflect similar policy preferences, and they may reflect other limitations as well. They may suffer from class, gender, and ethnicity biases..."*

From this qualified observation and common sense, we can realistically conjecture that bias exists in all national court systems and they have particular merits and demerits. Where parties wish to engage in international business, it makes sense to choose a jurisdiction and a venue for resolution of conflicts in contract matters in a place that has well-established commercial law and fair practices. For such purposes, major trading cities and towns in major world economies practicing rule of law, such as the major metropolises of New York, London, Manchester, Paris, Geneva, Berlin, Singapore, Tokyo, Hong Kong, etc., would on the face of it seem ideal. However, there are issues of bias and perceived bias. In the United States they believe they have a good judicial system. In the author's experience, in legal matters, US businesses deem the UK courts to be generally unbiased. However, they generally don't hold French and German courts in the same regard, will avoid being subject to their jurisdiction and are fearful of being denied the right to a jury-based trial. Within Europe, judicial equivalency and mutual recognition is a condition of EU membership. Romanic Law is the dominant legal system and though all courts still exhibit their own nationalistic idiosyncrasies and biases there is a gradual movement to harmonisation of law and judicial standards. Whether real or not, the perception of national prejudice in a continental court would fill many a businessman from an Anglo-Saxon economy with dread, but bias aside, there are some real merits in the code-based system. One such advantage is on the issue of good faith. It was an important concept and cornerstone in late Roman law and pre-codification medieval French Law, and as such its presumption in contract law is widely enshrined in national civic-law codes of countries deriving their law from the Romanic system. Hence, in much of Europe, Latin America and those of the major economies of the Far East who have adopted their commercial law practice from German law codes, generally the default position of contract law is that good faith is presumed[44]. By far the greatest advantage of code-based law is time and legal expense. For example, in patent litigation issues, say for a medium-risk case where US$1 million to US$25 million is at jeopardy, typical costs would be in the ranges:

- Europe: €100,000–375,000

- United Kingdom: €150,000–1.5 million

- United States: $650,000–2.5 million

In the US, 60% of costs are for the pre-trial 'discovery' process and above US$25 million at jeopardy, costs can more than double. Thus, if you are a British, North American or even a Commonwealth businessman standing before a French or German court on a matter of litigation on a contractual matter, if you have adequately qualified local counsel, your case is based on fact and does not involve any sleight to Gallic or Germanic national pride, your chances for an unbiased trial and favourable outcome should be very good. However, don't wind-up the judge and don't disrespect national customs or you could be screwed.

Despite the general perception that the US has a good judicial system, there are a number of characteristics of their system and anomalies in its practice that pose significant risk to business. These are manifested through procedural and cultural judicial bias and criminal manipulation of due process, both within the US and given the tendency of the US to stretch its extrajudicial reach, to the wider world. Within the EU, including the United Kingdom, there has been a general trend for convergence of legal systems and standards of justice, and a mutual recognition of civil court rulings in all member states, with interactions being governed by Hague Conventions on Private International Law (HCCH, a.k.a. Hague Conference/Conférence de La Haye). Given the advantages offered of commonality in rule of law, these trends are highly likely to continue across all Europe even post Brexit.

7.5.2 The Non-equivalency of Custom and Practice in US and English Law

Of all national jurisdictions, the US stands out as an area of significant commercial risk from the perspective of legal issues. In particular, there are a number of structural issues within the legal system, the manner in which law is practiced and the culture within the legal profession that give rise to anomalies which have been exploited by clever attorneys seeking to game the US legal system. Such problems include:

- Vexatious and frivolous cases allowed into the courts despite 'hollow claims'.

- Non-compliance with Hague Convention.

- Court system turning a blind eye to 'blackmail by attorney'.

- Abuses of the discovery process.

- Manipulation of choice of venue to exploit jury bias.

When a complainant wishes to bring a civil case in the courts in England and Wales, they must first file papers with the County Court (for claims up to £15,000) or optionally the High Court (for claims above £15,000). The complainant (or plaintiff) is required to put forward details of his complaint on how it has arisen with prima facia evidence of the claims against the other party, their validity in law and provide details of any injuries or damage caused by the incident. The court then examines the complaint, to see if it meets sufficient evidential standards to warrant court proceedings. If the court finds that a case meets pleading standards and to be arguable, the plaintiff's papers are served on the other party, who becomes the defendant in the proceedings. The defendant typically has three months to respond to the complaint, during which time he may file a counter action, seek to have the case thrown out on its lack of merit or simply not defend the case. Once the 90 days is up and in the absence of a motion to dismiss the complaint for lack of merit, the judge usually sets a time limit on the parties to seek documentary evidence of each other under the court's powers, then the case proceeds to trial. In the UK discovery is usually three to six months, with overall timeframes for litigation being one to two years.

In the US Federal Court system there are some critical differences in proceedings: When a complainant wishes to bring a civil case in the US courts, the court makes no assessment on the merits of the pleading as filed by the plaintiff. Once received by the court, the papers are automatically served on the other party – and the documents are automatically put into the public domain (and available worldwide on the web) – in some cases before the other party officially receives them. Once both parties have had their chance to respond, the judge sets an initial hearing date. If the defendant hasn't responded, doesn't show up or is not represented in court, at the plaintiff's request the judge can issue a judgement in default against the defendant – without even examining the merits of the case and its basis in law, if he/she so chooses. In most other jurisdictions worldwide, at this stage the case would be examined in detail and the viability of the plaintiff's claim tested.

In the US, if the defendant responds with a motion to dismiss the case on its merits, the judge probably for the first time examines the case. However, he/she cannot treat the parties equally under the law at this stage and purely for the purposes of motions to dismiss, unless otherwise 100% provably not a fact, the judge must take 'any' statement made by the defendant as 'fact in law', even if unsupported by corroborative evidence. Thus, a suitably motivated attorney (paid by the hour at US$300 to $700/ hour) can easily craft a complaint that cannot be dismissed. Where the case survives the motion to dismiss, then the judge commences the discovery process. In the US, the laws on discovery are much stronger than in any other jurisdiction, and the process will usually take a further six months to two years. However, there have been cases of such acrimony in the US courts that the discovery process had gone on for eight years, which, at an estimated cost of circa US$1 million p.a. to each party, is a hefty legal cost. As an American friend once told me, *"Your national game is Cricket, but ours is Poker!"*, illustrating the point that an unethical attorney can game the system to stretch out discovery and ramp up costs to *'up the ante'*, to the point where the opposition will throw in the towel, by settling out of court or choosing to accept judgement in default. Some litigants, particularly in alleged patent troll cases will file their lawsuit against multiple parties, some of whom will settle even frivolous or vexatious claims to minimise overall costs to their companies. The plaintiff will then use the funds he has obtained from those who settle to fund the ongoing case against those who don't. Provided more defendants settle than don't, the plaintiff will be cash richer, even if he loses the case at the end of proceedings. The general public would deem these behaviours as reprehensible, but in the US it's a perfectly legal strategy and would not be subject of judicial or professional reprimand. Even if a motion to dismiss is successful, the defendant's legal costs will typically be in the range US$50,000 to US$100,000. If not, and the case has to go to discovery for it to be revealed it has no merit, two years later the costs will be circa US$500,000 to US$600,000. At this point, though with no valid case, unless the plaintiff can be proven to have deliberately sought a vexatious litigation, there will be no possibility of recovery of costs, and the plaintiff and his attorney can simply walk away saying, *"Sorry, we thought we had a case but it turned out not to be a strong as we thought."*

So, for a belligerent litigant set on 'gaming the system', the US courts can provide a mechanism for legally facilitated blackmail, which would not be possible in any other jurisdiction. Naturally this possibility has occurred to the US judiciary and there have been several investigations into judicial practices, by (guess who) attorneys and the judiciary. The general consensus is that there is no wide-scale abuse of the system. But let's get real here, folks. This is a profession that annually disbars one in 1,000 of its members for criminal or unethical wrongdoing, and who are portrayed in popular US culture as blood-sucking parasites, liars, facilitators of organised crime and even as the devil incarnate. Only in the US are attorneys held in such contempt by the general public; elsewhere in the world the law is a respected profession to be aspired to. In the US, when presented with a difficult to dismiss a vexatious complaint, the defendant's attorney is frequently called up by the plaintiff's attorney who offers to *"make the case 'go away' for a price"*. This is so-called 'go-away money'. In the US the defendant's attorney will usually advise his client to save years of aggravation and stress, and settle out of court without admitting liability. These no-fault, out-of-court settlements between the parties are covered by 'nondisclosure agreements', and any discussions of them or negotiations between the parties relating to potential settlement are deemed privileged, and as such not admissible in court, even if associated with threats and admissions by the plaintiff's attorney, *"Yes, I know my client doesn't have a case, but we're filing anyway"*. Thus, the magnitude of this practice is virtually invisible to the US authorities, and rendered so by US law. From personal experience and knowing several parties who found themselves in similar positions, the current rate for 'go-away' money is circa $600,000, with $500,000 going to the plaintiff, and the rest to his attorney. The plaintiff's attorney's proposition is simple, *"You're going to have to pay this out anyway, even if we lose, so save yourself a lot of grief and avoid the chance you'll lose and end up paying more."* The defendant has a choice, to fight and pay costs or give in to blackmail. The responses to such offers are culturally driven, but most US defendants will settle out of economic pragmatism, whereas most Brits and Germans will be minded to fight even if it costs. Russians, on the other hand, will fight, and coming from a culture that hasn't a strong tradition of settling disputes in court, they might even be minded to have the other party's attorney killed. You would think that such cultural variances might faze US attorneys when advising their clients to litigate, but alas not. Most US attorneys have scant international cross cultural business experience compared to their European counterparts and will assume that a foreign party will behave in the same cultural way and economically rational manner as a US party.

Whilst the above is a single personal view from outside the US, what do Americans actually think about their legal system? A study conducted by Harvard Law School published in 2010[45] found the comparative national litigation rates:

International Measure of Litigation – 2010

Country	Suits Filed per 100,000 Population	Comparative %
USA	5806	100.0
UK	3681	63.4
France	2416	41.6
Japan	1768	30.5
Australia	1542	26.6
Canada	1450	25.0

It would be anticipated that UK litigation rates would be disproportionately high, as London is the world's premier seat for settling international disputes. A 2015 survey of UK and European law firms operating in the UK conducted by the British Institute of International and Comparative Law for the Ministry of Justice[46] concluded:

"A factor often stressed by respondents was that English courts had successfully established themselves as the default jurisdiction for parties that had unsatisfactory judicial and/or legal systems in their home jurisdictions or where, in the view of both parties, the choice of English courts was the acceptable compromise solution."

The survey makes note of the observation in relation to UK litigation that:

"Half of respondents stated that more than 60% of their cases in the last five years were cross-border claims, with a quarter nearly exclusively doing cross-border work (90–100%)."

Thus we can conclude that exclusively domestic litigation rates for the UK lie somewhat closer to those of Japan, Canada and Australia. Yet per capita, the number of cases that actually make it into the courtroom post the discovery process in both the US and UK jurisdictions are comparable. Thus, the above implies that well over a half of the cases filed in the US are unnecessary and potentially frivolous or veracious cases.

According to the Chamber of US Legal Reform, the costs of tort litigation are staggering, especially for small businesses, where the tort liability costs in 2008 were an eye-watering US$105.4 billion[47]. According to then (now former) Congressman Terry Everett when speaking of government reform in 2009, *"Frivolous lawsuits alone are said to cost the United States $200 billion a year and all of these potentially unwarranted claims are having an effect on how Americans view the legal system."* This view was validated at the time by a survey conducted by Harris Interactive[48] that found:

- 76% of those surveyed felt that fear of frivolous lawsuits discouraged people from performing normal activities.

- Only 16% trusted the legal system to defend them against frivolous lawsuits.

- 54% did not trust the legal system.

- 67% strongly agreed (and 27% somewhat agreed) that there was an increasing tendency for people to threaten legal action when something went wrong.

- 83% felt that the legal system made it too easy to make invalid claims.

- 56% thought that there were fundamental changes needed to make the civil justice system work better.

- 55% strongly agreed (and another 32% somewhat agreed) that the justice system was used by many as a lottery, to start a lawsuit and see just how much they could win.

If that's what the average US citizen feels, then who are we to contradict them? Notwithstanding the US judicial system's 'Nelson's eye' view of its systemic abuse, owing to public pressure on the legislature, there have been attempts to improve the poor standards of US court pleadings, notably in the form of The Lawsuit Abuse Reduction Act (H.R. 758) which has just passed its second reading in the House and is now at its Senate Committee stage. Notably this act seeks to withdraw the right of an attorney to file 'any old complaint' and publicly slander a defendant with total impunity via the court system, and have up to 21 days to amend that complaint. It will strengthen judicial sanction for breaches of pleading rules, notably Rule 11(b) on the veracity and intent of pleadings, which my own attorney had noted "*is more observed in the breach than the compliance*". It is notable that at present, for deliberately violating rule

11(b) other than a verbal reprimand by the judge and a derisory fine of typically less than US$10,000 for the unethical attorney, there are no monetary penalties that can be levied on represented clients bringing a frivolous or vexatious lawsuit. Given the sums at stake, and such pathetic response by the judiciary to brazen fraud in the courtroom via abuse of process, it's no wonder public dissatisfaction with the system is widespread in the US. The proposed changes to statute won't do anything to address the imbalance in standing between parties in motions to dismiss and it won't address the absurdity of the cost and duration of the discovery process, which are only necessary because the court allows such weak and uncorroborated pleadings as an initial complaint to be filed in the first instance. Thus, whilst the act may slightly reduce frivolous claims, it still won't preclude attorneys from abusing the system and the use of the same for *'legalised blackmail'*.

There are added complications with regard to US international document service. Service of legal papers internationally is governed by the Hague Convention on Document Service. It requires the courts in the nation seeking service to do so in full accordance with the procedures of service of documents in the receiving party's country. Thus, papers raised in the US and served in England and Wales must comply with English law's terms of service. However, the reality is that in a US Federal Court, papers whether national or internationally are served in accordance with Federal Law, irrespective of which nation they are served in and whether its terms of service differ, and the clerk of the US court will issue a docket stamped *'Served in Accordance with the Hague Convention'*, whether he knows it was a compliant service or not. Worse still, if the legality of service is subsequently challenged as being improper through a breach of the convention's terms, there is judicial precedent in US Federal Court rejecting improper service as grounds against the action proceeding as if it service was proper. As observed by Benvenisti and Downs the US courts like others are *"agents of their states, and more often than not reflect similar policy preferences..."*, and the US political and cultural aversion to the rule of law other than their own domestic legislation can transcend obligations in international treaties and laws, and in doing so, the US courts have no qualms about effectively 'giving the finger' to external jurisdictions.

The terms of service of legal papers on British companies has been defined over many years to ensure proper service is made such that the company is alerted to the legal action and can take appropriate measures and avoid a judgment in default. Given the US practice on Hague and its propensity and manner of issuing judgments in default, there is a real possibility that a UK entity could find itself on the wrong end of a US Court judgment in default, which it does not know of and may not have had notice of until it is past time to appeal. The vulnerability of UK companies to this hazard is rendered real by virtue of the UK government's decision to recognise US court rulings on civil matters with regard to enforcement of money awards. The risk to British companies is further magnified by the treatment of foreign court rulings by UK courts: The English court will generally not '*look behind the judgment*' of the foreign court[49]. The decision cannot be set aside on its merits, either of fact or of law, even if the English court can be satisfied that the decision of the foreign court is wrong as a matter of law. Thus, the possibility of appealing against any foreign judgment in the UK is very improbable. For a foreign judgment to be recognised, all that is required is that:

- The judgment is final and conclusive on the merits, to which the US courts will attest but the UK court will not validate, as it won't '*look behind the judgment*'.

- The claim is for a specific, definite amount of money including a final order for costs, rather than a specific performance, i.e. they can demand monies, but not assets or performance.

117

- The foreign court had jurisdiction according to English rules, which in the US' case the Blair government gave away.

In contrast, the US government (citing difficulties in their constitution), do not reciprocate recognition of rulings of foreign national courts by any bilateral or multilateral treaty[50]. The courts of some US states will hear applications for recognition of foreign country court rulings, on the basis of judge-made law or local statute, a primary condition for which being that the awarding foreign national court had 'personal jurisdiction' over the US defendant against whom the award was made. This means that any non-US party having successfully litigated in their own non-US jurisdiction will have to re-present and possibly re-fight their case again in the relevant US state court, more than doubling the cost outlay, effectively precluding effective enforcement of any case against a US company or individual obtained outside the US, and could only do so if the US defendant had effective dual national status or previously recognised the foreign jurisdiction in the matter. Several US states will not recognise enforcement of judgements in default, even those obtained in other US states, on grounds that such awards are questionable. Yet we have a ludicrous situation the UK courts will recognise any US court award, even judgments in default, without looking behind them.

The decision to recognise US Civil courts in the UK was freely offered by the former Blair government to the Bush administration without reciprocation. This was in the run-up to the Iraq war and supposedly to help cement the Anglo-UK 'Special Relationship', on the purported grounds of the equivalency of the UK and US judicial systems.

The reality is the UK and US legal systems are far from equivalent, with the non-equivalency of standing of parties in the US thrown into stark relief when attorneys for US parties will make note in court papers and oral argument of the 'foreign national' status of their opponents in a bid to prejudice proceedings, especially in relation to proposed jury trial. Similar comment in any European court would be treated with utter incredulity, and perhaps be incredulous to the reader. However, I would direct the reader to examine the pronouncements of Donald Trump during his 2016 presidential campaign, and reflect on the strength of populism that antiforeigner rhetoric can engender in working-class middle America, and think what purpose an unscrupulous attorney could do to manipulate the same.

There is significant evidence of manipulation of the jury process in the federal court system, in the behaviour of alleged patent trolls seeking to domicile their headquarters (at least on paper), in low population rural federal court districts. For example, consider recent events in the Eastern District of Texas, centring on Marshall, Texas (population under 24,000, and principal industry: insurance claims processing), where in 2013, 24.5% of the US's 6,000 patent lawsuits were filed. Other than a plentiful supply of 'rednecks', who might be more amenable to patentees' rights and be more independently minded to resist compliance with national federal court guidelines, what possible reason can there be for such a concentration of cases involving a high level of technical and legal complexity, in a region where the average jury panellist would be well out of their depth?

Prior to ceding unchallengeable British recognition of US civil court judgments, Blair, much criticised over the Iraq war debacle, was a barrister and had never been a business practitioner. Some might even say given his professed desire for Britain to adopt the euro and the growth in income inequality over his three terms as prime minister, he wasn't any great shakes in matters of business, change management and economics, and as such he was hardly capable of understanding the non-equivalency of UK-US legal practice and its potential adverse economic impact on UK business. To quote Lord Haskins, one of Tony Blair's *"favourite businessmen"*, and key business adviser to No. 10, in the Blair years, Blair was *"not a big political thinker"* and that he was

119

"*not interested in delivery*"[51]. As a consequence of Blair's lack of insight and foresight, the exposure of UK companies to US civil courts awards arising from vexatious and frivolous litigation brought by unethical attorneys and patent trolls has radically increased, due to the unethical and criminal hazards posed by the way law is practiced in the US, and its risk to businesses beyond its borders.

7.6 Dispute Resolution, Arbitration and Its Subversion.

Given the spectrum of legal custom and practice worldwide, with different business cultures and even with the vagaries of language, all of which can potentially increase business risk and legal costs, any rational person would come to the conclusion that there has to be a simple and mutually beneficial way of settling legal disputes between commercial entities. The reality is that there is – arbitration, which takes any dispute out of the courtroom to resolve it in a pragmatic low-cost and faster route. The parties can choose which laws will pertain to their agreement, the venue and manner in which the dispute will be resolved. In doing so, they can circumvent the need to go to the courts, thereby saving time and expense. Arbitration has proven to be so successful at the national level that governments combined to draft the 1958 Convention on the Recognition and Enforcement of Foreign Arbitration Awards (the New York Convention), thereby creating a vehicle by which arbitration of as process can be practiced and its outcomes enforced internationally within any nation that is a signatory to the convention.

Given that English is the *lingua franca* of business worldwide, and London with its multi-ethnic culture and commercial history is one of the foremost if not the foremost international trading city in the world, arbitration under the rules of the London Court of International Arbitration (LCIA)[52], with London as its seat and conducted under English law has become a worldwide standard for the resolution of international business disputes. Also, given that the only way of having an arbitration ruling overturned is to prove the process wasn't impartial, the LCIA is utterly meticulous in its proceedings to the point that if the parties in dispute are from different countries and there is a sole arbiter, that arbiter may not be from either country of the parties in dispute.

As of 2015, there were 153 signatories to the New York Convention encompassing most of the developed and developing world outside Africa. Even the US ratified the convention in 1970. Typically, costs of LCIA arbitration are less than one tenth of going to law in the US, timescales more than halved and the disputes are resolved in a closed forum. Such are the advantages of LCIA arbitration that even in cases where both parties in dispute were US based or both from the Far East, they have chosen to arbitrate in London under English law. As of 2015 London was the seat for 45% of all international arbitration cases[53]. Within the US, awards made under equitable arbitration as per the LCIA can't be overturned or disputed, and are backed by the provisions of the New York Convention as if they were an Act of Congress. A properly drafted equitable dispute resolution clause in international business contracts can eradicate any cultural bias and largely circumvent the risks posed by US law and unethical legal practices, and avoid the need to air dirty linen in public. The above being said, a ruthless and clever attorney will always try to find a way to 'game the system'.

In circumstances where a dispute arises between two parties, one US based and the other non-US domiciled, and both have prior contracted to an equitable dispute resolution process as defined by US Congress, it makes sense to follow the contracted procedure to arbitrate, for all the reasons given above. However, the US party has the right to initiate legal proceedings in the federal courts to overturn the obligation to go to arbitration, even though such efforts will be ultimately unsuccessful. Consequently, the other party will have to answer the suit or risk an erroneous judgement in default. The tactics used by the US party can involve, where the contracting parties are companies, adding defendant company's officers to the lawsuit, claiming they were also acting in their personal capacity or that the behaviours of these officers were contrary to public statute, e.g. were criminally fraudulent. In jurisdictions outside the US such accusations would be deemed very serious indeed and the judge would seek evidence that any such charges had a foundation. Inside the US such accusations in business disputes are *de rigueur* and would not be tested by the judge until post discovery. With such a stratagem the US party could potentially obviate their obligation to arbitrate and maintain a case in the federal court. Why try to maintain the high-cost legal option to dispute resolution? It's difficult to make a demand of US$600,000, in 'go-away' money when all you have are hollow claims and the defendant can fend off the attack for a tenth of that cost in arbitration.

In relation to the point of use of cost as a weapon: Almost all dispute resolution procedures involve the option of mediation prior to any instigation of formal arbitration; however, standards in practice vary widely across the world. In one circumstance I came across in a dispute between a US company and one of its contractors with US$150,000 in unpaid back fees due to the contractor, both parties agreed to mediation rather than going to law. A professional mediator and venue was arranged, the contractor and his attorney showed up, but the company didn't, cancelling at the very last moment on the day of the meeting. The cost to the contractor for mediator, venue and his attorney's time was US$10,000. The mediator rescheduled everything for a few weeks later and lo and behold another no-show. The mediator simply rescheduled and events were repeated more than a half dozen times in all. At which point some US$70,000 out of pocket, the contractor settled for a US$40,000 *ex-gratia* payment from the firm, whose cost to that point had been for a mere handful of phone calls by its attorney. The same US company, represented by the same attorney repeated the same late cancellation trick in court proceedings and the judge simply issued a default judgement against them for non-appearance. In the US, mediation and judicial standards in general and especially so at state court level are highly variable in quality and certainty of outcome.

Clearly there are increased commercial risks in doing business in the US owing to the vagaries of their legal system and above all its ludicrous costs. Dispute resolution procedures encompassing mediation and arbitration are essential in all contracts covering business proceedings. However, when drafting arbitration clauses, they must be equitable, robust and for dealings involving US parties, they have to be made as circumvention proof as possible. The US should be avoided with regard to being the seat of any mediation, arbitration or legal proceeding in any international dispute, and it would be preferable that the law pertaining to any part of the contract be anything other than US law or jurisdiction, thereby avoiding any recourse of any party to the US courts. I would recommend ensuring that company officers are safeguarded by making them party to arbitration in their personal as well as their formal capacity as representatives of the company. I would also ensure that any party who seeks to circumvent prior contracted arbitration is contractually obligated to bear full legal costs for all parties in any related proceedings.

7.7 Negotiation – Robust and Over-Robust

Negotiation is the crux of formation of contract and even the avoidance of disputes in business dealings. I well remember extensive negotiation training during my MBA, with the emphasis being on trying to obtain a win-win solution for all parties. However, real life is far from the perceived ideals of academia and industrial relations idealists. In the real world when you meet fraudsters, High-P individuals or just the downright unethical, who don't perceive a need for an ongoing relationship, their objective priorities are: WIN-LOSE, WIN-lose, WIN-win and at worst win-lose. This class of people do not want equanimity, they want to win and win bigger than the other party even if the other party loses. This is especially so in situations where the deal being negotiated is a one-off; either the sale of an asset or an irrevocable right. The bigger the disparity the better they feel and if that means they win big and you lose big, so be it. And typically they don't care what you will think of them after the event, they just want to win and get one over on the other party.

When negotiating with a party who desires an inequitable solution, it's imperative you know where they're coming from. The egocentric High-P individual will be drawn – not just by greed – but the thrill he gets in the kill of sealing the deal and the trophy value he can display to his acolytes. You might consider that it's almost impossible to deal with such individuals and admittedly it is difficult at best. You could potentially deal with these issues by building in perceived trophy value and augment the haggling experience for the High-P opponent to feel empowered. On one occasion I came across, the High-P individual, fancied himself the ladies' man. The executives who needed his sanction on a deal took him out to an expensive restaurant to be wined and dined. After the meal they adjourned to a local bar, whereupon the High-P individual predictably mixed and flirted with everything in a skirt, and in front of the assembled entourage he seemed to be doing very well. By the end of the evening he had pulled two attractive ladies much younger than himself, and rather than go back to his hotel, he went back to their place. The next morning, the smug High-P individual was happy to conclude negotiations whilst being able to brag about his threesome and general prowess with women. However, unbeknownst to him, the ladies in question were prostitutes, targeted and pre-paid for a full night's work.

I once said to a man with whom I had business dealings and whom I later found out to be a career criminal fraudster, *"You'd rather steal ten cents than earn an honest dollar through less effort"*. He was initially taken aback at my bluntness, but I could see his genuine reflection on his actions which had led to my comment, and he replied in all seriousness, *"You know what? You're right, but I just can't help myself, I get such a buzz out of it"*. The same guy had on occasions been manipulated by others in 'packing a deal' through them to apparently allow themselves to be defrauded of just enough for the miscreant to fulfil his emotional need to feel he'd cheated and won. On that occasion he purchased a company, paying US$4 million in an exchange of stock, thinking he'd got the better of the deal because the realisable value of the stock he handed over was less than US$2 million – but he was the one ultimately defrauded as the company he purchased was worth nothing.

In situations where you can't appease the High-P individual by feeding their ego or offering crumbs as metaphoric trophies it's better to either just slug it out to see what you can get but ultimately be prepared to walk away. Situations where you should immediately walk away are those where you detect:

(a) **Criminal intent**: Where there is criminal intent to defraud, there is no win option for your party. That's the whole purpose of stealing and defrauding; it's not the sort of relationship where win-win is possible.

126

(b) Intimidation: There are those who seek to obtain the advantage in negotiation by bullying and browbeating opponents into taking weaker positions through bearing, and an intimidatory posture. Worse still, some will even resort to threats of violence.

When someone is trying to negotiate a deal or resolve a dispute through bullying or worse, if you're the type intimidated by such posture and mind games, you have to walk away. If you're not the type of person to be intimidated, it's still advisable you walk away, as there's no comfortable way in which you can appease that type of psychological need in the other party.

One should not confuse bullying with what a lawyer might perceive as 'robust' business negotiation. In business meetings, particularly those relating to complaints and disputes, passions can be raised and points of view forcefully exchanged. There may even be threats made, for example, if your firm doesn't comply with our demands we'll litigate or strike you from our suppliers list and those of our group companies. They might even say, *"We'll never speak to you again."* Body language might become aggressive, and even tables banged with fists to emphasise determination or defiance. But there is a line, when passion becomes 'over-robust' business negotiation. That line gets crossed into the realms of criminal threatening (or threatening behaviour) when the assailing party intentionally or knowingly puts another person in fear of bodily injury or mental damage, or a material and detriment or loss. It is all well and good to threaten a company's representative that you will take his company to court, but it's quite another to say to him or her, *"I'm going to destroy you"* or *"I'm going to ruin you and see your family on the street."* It's also beyond the pale to issue thinly veiled threats of personal violence e.g., *"We know some very nasty guys in our business, so you don't want to cross us"*. Such threats can of course seem childish to a mature adult, but they cease to be so when you discover the other party does actually have associations with organised crime. Under such conditions, threatening behaviour associated with a menacing demand quite literally becomes blackmail, and where provable moves from the realm of a civil dispute to the police and criminal justice system. Penalties for blackmail are largely culturally dependent. In the US, penalties are comparatively light for such, and for the most part they are treated as a misdemeanour. Outside the jurisdiction of US, penalties in most developed nations for similar behaviour can range from one to two years from minor transgressions to five years to 25 years where menaces are involved, and in the case of Saudi Arabia they'll throw in 150 lashes onto sentences in the same range. It is my experience that there is an inverse correlation between the penalty for blackmail in any jurisdiction (an index of its cultural acceptance) and the propensity to threaten in over-robust business negotiation.

Those who make such threats are usually from business cultures where such conduct might even be perceived as normal, and 'just business', and in some circumstances in such cultures it's not unheard of that an individual might wave a blunt instrument (e.g. a hammer) or even produce a large hand gun. Where such threats occur, and they do occur, in my experience they are perpetrated in such a forum that the perpetrator can deny the threat. This could happen on the perpetrator's own premises, an informal face-to-face setting away from attorneys (well, yours at least), note takers and recording devices. Some even take place over the phone. Business takes place over the globe and there are many regions in the world where fraud and crime are endemic. These are precisely the sort of areas that the businessman is faced with increased risk of over-robust negotiation tactics and must take adequate precautions regarding (a) physical safety and (b) electronically recording events.

Recording business dealings over the phone can be problematic in the US principally because 11 of the 50 states have some legislation requiring all-party consent. Thus, if you make a phone recording of someone from a US state that requires all-party consent threatening you with violence and attempting to blackmail you, they may be found guilty of an offence and be fined and get a year in jail. You, on the other hand, might also get fined up to US$10,000 and one to three years in jail, just for taping them. There is a general belief that the all-party consent laws in the US can provide a veil behind which fraudsters and blackmailers can thrive and there is some evidence for that. WalletHub's analysts compared the 50 states and the District of Columbia (DC) for their vulnerability to identity theft and fraud[54], ranking states in accordance to an index encompassing complaints per 100,000 residents relating to identity theft, government-documents or -benefits fraud, credit-card fraud, phone or utilities fraud, bank fraud, employment fraud, cybercrime-related dollar losses per capita, and number of data breaches. Of the ten worst performing states in the index's ranking, six have, or recently had, all-party consent requirement laws for telephone recording. It is not unreasonable to assume that ethics practiced in business are a reflection of the surrounding ethical culture of society; after all, the former is born from, and constantly interacting with, the latter. As such the index, whilst not perfect, is an indicator of where business culture might put a party at risk of encountering 'over-robust' negotiation as a cultural style; it should put a party on notice to take extra care in doing business in greater Chicago, greater New York (including Connecticut), southwestern US (California, Nevada, Arizona) and Florida. It should also be noted at that certain localities in the US, though well documented, are not the only regions of the world where you'll find thugs and organised crime actively engaged in what appear to be legitimate businesses.

Where over-robust negotiation is encountered, it should be documented or recorded, line management or colleagues should be advised. Where criminality is suspected, these should be advised to the company secretary and the company's legal counsel, and a proper risk assessment should be made and acted upon. Where there are threats of violence, these should be advised to the police as a complaint and a formal crime number recorded in the company's archive. Should the very worst happen and someone tries to make good on the threat, the evidence will be at hand.

8. Business Strategy and the Art of Dirty War

8.1 The Boundary between Legality and Criminality

In considering the strategic implications of unethical and criminal conduct, it is essential to have clarity of understanding on the meaning of ethics. Firstly we can take it as read that what is criminal is that action or behaviour deemed illegal by statute and law. In Anglo-Saxon law, everything that isn't specifically prohibited in statute and law is legal. However, there are aspects of criminal codes that at least sections of the wider public deem as not unethical to violate, for example, downloading copyright materials from the internet, pro bono. Ethics is more nebulous a subject, being defined as moral principles that govern a person's behaviour or the conducting of an activity. In many cases ethical standards will evolve over time and frequently law will take time to catch up with the actuality of conventional lives, thereby creating a gap between what the public deem as ethical, but the law deems illegal. For example, the evolution of the Western public's attitude toward LGBT issues, in relation to legislation relating to the same from the period of the mid-20th century to the present. The boundaries of ethics will largely be a function of one's culture and even religious persuasion.

Figure 4 – The Boundary Between Legality and Criminality

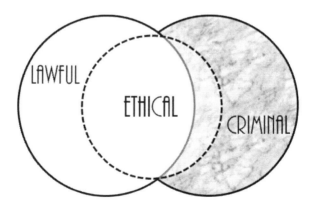

For simplistic purposes, what is ethical may be interpreted as what would be deemed 'right and proper' in the eyes of the wider public. Yet in practice there is another corporate definition of ethics and it can be defined as obeying laws and regulations and visibly complying with the same. Quite clearly there is some discrepancy between what a corporation might decide is ethical and the stance of the wider public. Thus a Western corporation might offshore its manufacture to a company in a developing nation that employs sweat labour working under poorer but legal local conditions that would be illegal in the West. This of course is entirely legal and if properly conducted, an ethical corporation could legally say it had complied with all requisite legislation. But the matter is not so clear cut in the eyes of the public. Take this example: In 2005, a survey conducted by Ethical Consumer magazine, found that only five UK high-street brands scored 10 or over out of 20 assessing their ethical standards. Primark was alleged to be the worst offender, according to the survey, with a score of 2.5. It was followed by Mk One, at 3 points, with Marks & Spencer, Debenhams and Gap filling out the bottom five. The report was based on data on thousands of different companies, supplied by various environmental and labour activist groups then compiled by Ethical Consumer magazine. Yet to my knowledge, none of these companies has ever been prosecuted for any criminality in any jurisdiction in relation to its supply-chain practices. Quite clearly there is a perception gap between corporations and citizens as to what is unethical. For the purposes of this text, we consider that the view of what isn't socially acceptable shall constitute 'unethical conduct', even if legal in the eyes of the law. Thus there are four types of organisations:

(1) **The 'truly ethical organisation'** – Stays both within the bounds of what is legal and what is deemed acceptable by wider society.

(2) The 'legally ethical organisation' – May stray from the expectations of societal norms, but stays within the bounds of what is lawful by criminal statute.

(3) The 'unethical organisation' – Regularly fails to meet the expectations of societal norms, and may occasionally stray into the realms of criminality.

(4) The 'criminal organisation' – Routinely breaches criminal statute, and may be classified as an organised criminal enterprise.

The very existence of this grey area between legality and ethicality, 'in and of itself' is a significant feature of the ethics landscape that can be exploited by the unethical business.

8.2 Battle Strategies

There are many books on corporate strategy, and the basic teaching texts recommended at degree and masters level give more than most executives will need in their careers[55,56,57,58]. However, they do little to prepare the naïve young marketer for their first encounter with unethical conduct, and in some cases, downright criminality they will inevitably encounter when they enter the 'real world'. As with all higher education courses, the value obtained from them for the student is to be found in widely reading the subject beyond the courses' core texts. When it comes to factoring in the criminal or unethical conduct of players in a market, most strategic management texts are found wanting.

When we consider the history of warfare, we can see repeated patterns and derive from them behavioural models with which we can predict future events. Hitler's infamous spymaster Reinhard Gehlen wrote in his memoirs: *"The essence of secret intelligence service, apart from an all-embracing knowledge, is the ability to follow and project trends into the future."* Thus, to expand our understanding of unethical conduct in strategic management, we have to seek '*all-encompassing knowledge*' and look beyond advanced marketing texts and read wider, of the real-world experiences in military and political history, history and politics, organisational behaviour and sociology, and even biographies of the rich and famous. Widely reading such texts shows the world in all its grim reality rather than an idealised academic construct.

8.2.1 The Belgium Sucker Punch

If we examine the military history of the German invasion of France in WWI, as most school children will know, the Germans threw the rule book on the customs and practice of war out of the window and in 1914 attacked France, bypassing the heavily defended French-German border by invading through neutral Belgium's Ardennes. In doing so, the Germans breached their obligations in international law to respect the neutrality of non-belligerent states as inviolable, as agreed under the Hague Convention of 1907. An undeniably unethical and criminal act, but one that yielded massive tactical advantages in terms of surprising their enemy and being able to focus their attack on their opponent's weakest defences. Post WWI, under the 1919 Treaty of Paris, war criminals were to be tried in international courts for their crimes. The allies submitted a list of 900 names to the German government, but their extradition to face trial on foreign soil was refused. The Germans agreed to try the alleged criminals in their own courts. The allies submitted a much-reduced list of 45 names. Most could not be found and only a handful were ever tried and convicted (at the Leipzig War Trials in 1921) and they received only paltry sentences. Nobody was ever appropriately admonished for the ruin of Belgium. I would add that the war reparations loaded on Germany by France did not punish those guilty for WWI, rather they collectively punished the German people for the errors of their leaders, and in doing so spawned grievance and economic conditions to fuel further conflict.

As if to add insult to injury, history repeated itself in WWII, when in 1940, the Germans again attacked France via then-neutral Belgium and the Netherlands. Whilst the German underhandedness was great, the real medal for shame should be awarded to the French and British military leaders for ineptitude in not seeing the same 'sucker punch' coming the second time around. These historical events teach us many things about how organisations behave:

- The unethical or criminal organisation that throws away the rule book can exploit the ethics landscape and gain strategic advantage over ethical organisations. This is the 'Belgium sucker punch'.

- Rigid and blinkered thinking in market players and regulators alike impedes anticipation of breaches in ethics and preparation to deal with the unexpected.

- Without proper remedy, unethical and criminal behaviour will be reinforced and repeated.

Consider a modern-day attack on Europe and the Western world, this time from Germany's Volkswagen[59] (VW). In 2015 VW and a number of other carmakers were exposed for illegally cheating on diesel emissions tests, so that they could promote their diesel-powered cars in Europe and America as being greener than they were, and greener than their competitor's petrol engine cars. Some automakers exploited loopholes where emissions systems only operated within a specific temperature range so cars would perform better in lab testing, but emit more in the real world. The Financial Times reported US prosecutors as claiming knowledge of VW's cheating and 'defeat device' was widely known by VW management as early as 2006[60], with New York prosecutors alleging that VW had a "*stubborn and unrepentant culture*" that led to "*systematic cheating and deception*". Incredibly, EU regulators in Brussels were aware of temperature-based emissions manipulation as early as 2012, three years before VW's cheating was publicly exposed[61]. While this form of testing manipulation wasn't necessarily illegal (but clearly unethical in the eyes of the general public), it paints a poor picture of the cultural environment both within the company and the regulator that allowed VW to get away with breaking the law with its defeat devices. Thus once again history repeated itself, metaphorically at least, with

Germany's VW assailing the world car market via Belgium, by throwing away the rule book, in another example of the Belgium sucker punch.

To avoid the negative market consequences of the unethical or criminal abuse of the ethical landscape, the ethical organisation needs to:

- Take a wider view and expect the unexpected.

- Risk appraise foreseeable hazard and prepare contingency.

- Always play a straight game, such that when the unethical game plan fails and the regulator steps in, you are not implicated in any market shenanigans.

- Ensure that market regulators know what's going on in the real world beyond their offices in the capital.

8.2.2 Acing the Market

I first came upon the term 'acing the market' in the early 1990s, it had reputedly been coined in the commercial department of one of Europe's Big Six chemical companies of the time. An ace, in current times is the highest card in the pack and beats all others. People are familiar with the term to 'serve an ace' in tennis, where an ace is a legal serve, generally of such power and accuracy of placement that it cannot be touched by the receiver, winning the point for the server by effectively beating the opponent in one mighty stroke. So how does that translate to marketing? 'Acing the market' refers to a situation where a market player structures his product offer to market in a unique or exclusive way such that competitors are unable to respond to the market move or at least unable to respond in a timely enough manner to compete effectively, and thereby the server wins the available business. Critically, the situation of uniqueness created must be 'legal', such that the advantage achieved is tangible and not overturned by intervention of a market umpire, such as an industry regulator or governmental consumer watchdog. Examples of legitimate means of acing the market might include the successful launch of a new patented product, a unique disruptive innovation or a unique disruptive way of serving the market.

Back in the 1980s the Big Six major European chemical companies of the time had a commercial problem. The perception was that they were being undercut in the marketplace by lower-priced Indian and Chinese goods sold via much smaller EU-based traders. The Big Six viewed the Indians and Chinese as having inferior standards of manufacturing and quality which they assumed gave them a cost-based edge. The reality was that the European players were losing cost leadership, largely down to second-mover advantage of the Far Eastern competitors, who were designing out process problems the existing players lived with, and the emerging nations' products were in most cases at least as good. The Far Eastern competitors' advantages were not solely due to lower manufacturing operational costs, which in many cases were higher than in Europe, but to their lower administrative overheads, smarter purchasing and leaner sales distribution. In short, the Far Eastern new market entrants viewed the whole value chain with the same low-cost concept. The Big Six, though they squeezed manufacturing operation costs, were reluctant to rationalise their commercial arms, continuing to pay too many staff big salaries and high commissions. At the time, they had failed to appreciate the nature of the cost advantage of their non-EU competitors, and rather than address this cost differential and offer competitively within the marketplace, it was mooted that they could 'ace the market' by harnessing the EU's drive to create unity through centralisation and regulation.

The cynical reader joining the dots might reason, 'Ah, now I know why the REACH system[62] was born and why its rules and complexity are such a pain in the proverbial…' And most certainly the Far Eastern makers did view the regulation as a move to impose a trade barrier. Quite clearly, there was both a genuine need for control of potentially harmful substances and a political consensus for EU-wide intervention and regulation in this area. The Six conjectured that by instigating a system of increased regulatory compliance, not just on the manufacturing processes within the EU but on the products imported into it, with the cost burden falling upon the manufacturer or the primary importer into the EU, the SMEs that made up most of Europe's chemicals traders of Far Eastern products would be forced out of the market by the increased cost of the regulatory burden. In their game of cards, the European players were doubling up to force their competitors to fold. If successful, the EU majors would effectively bar many of their competitors' products from the EU market. After all, who wouldn't have their competitors' products taken off the market, if they could achieve the same lawfully? The aforementioned would of course be entirely legal as it would be the regulator who was acting to disenfranchise the non-EU competition and not the companies themselves, but was it legitimate or indeed ethical? As for the real impact on SME chemicals importers, the regulations did slowly achieve their 'purported' original design aim, and more. As collateral damage, they have almost eradicated the once highly profitable European-based small-scale fine chemicals sector, and added significant cost to the development of 'small molecule' pharmaceuticals (such as antibiotics) within Europe. This should be a salutary warning as to how in the best-made plans of mice and men things can go awry when instigators fail to understand the value chain and underestimate the full impact of letting the regulatory genie out of the bottle.

As further evidence for 'acing the market' by regulatory intervention, consider the contentious EU food standards regulations proposed or enacted over the last 20 years. Sausages – where large German-based producers of 'cooked meat' sausages sought to ban their raw meat competitor products. Ice-cream – where Italian manufacturers sought to disadvantage their competitors who made cheaper 'non-Italian recipe' products. Chocolate – where larger European-based confectionary manufacturers sought to disadvantage their non-animal fat based competitors by forcing them to use the name 'Vegelate' and influencing EC 2000/35 limiting vegetable fat to 5% or less (which is bad news for vegans). Bananas – where (though much exaggerated in the British press at the time) large corporate growers sought to influence the wholesale green banana market (through EC 2257/94) by instituting the specification of banana classification to favour the genetically uniform cloned hybrid cultivar 'musa cavendishii', and thus disadvantage their smaller competitors growing genetically less uniform and irregular bananas. And the list goes on and on. At its peak, some 36 fruits and vegetables had specific EU marketing standards. Through consumer and national government push-back this has now been reduced to 10, but why does the EU with borders stretching from within the Arctic circle of northern Finland and Sweden to southern Spain and Greece need a single standard for strawberries?

Consider the specifics of still EU-regulated strawberries, where large-scale poly-tunnel technology and modern hybrid growers have pressured for an EU specification of a minimum size of a strawberry of 18 mm in diameter (EC 543/2011), thereby raising the waste levels and costs of smaller-scale open field and heritage cultivar growers. What aspect of health and safety or consumer protection is promulgated by the setting of a minimum diameter of a strawberry? Is its taste inferior if less than 18 mm? Is it of less nutritional value or does it pose a choking hazard to small children? What the detail of the EU specification does do is act as an invisible barrier to trade, greatly reducing the number of growers who can economically deliver the exacting EU specification. Furthermore, it reduces the variety of cultivars grown and offered into the market, and that can't be in the best interest of the consumer or indeed good for long-term plant health and food security.

At one point the European Commission proposed a *Plant Reproductive Material Law* (EC 2013/137) which would have made it illegal to *"grow, reproduce or trade"* any vegetable seeds that have not been *"tested, approved and accepted"* by a new EU bureaucracy named the *"EU Plant Variety Agency."* In essence home gardeners and traders in small-scale 'heritage crops' who grow their own plants from non-regulated seeds would have been considered criminals or compelled to face massive costs of testing and regulatory approval. Many commercial heritage seed banks feared closure and the enforced destruction of the invaluable DNA resource banks they protected. Again, the question has to be asked, what aspect of health and safety or consumer protection is achieved by the total centralised government control of every food crop species? Whilst I see the health and safety need to regulate introduction of new species and GMO crops in particular, like many, I can't see the necessity for such all-encompassing legislation to govern existing food crops. However, for large-scale agrochemical and biotechnology corporations selling bulk seed such a directive could close down competition from inter-farmer trading and greatly expand their market share of the seed business.

When one examines the minutia of EU regulations with the question firmly in mind as what is served by the detail therein, the more it becomes difficult not to conclude that many EU directives have been highjacked by large commercial entities who by subtle amendment of regulation have sought to 'ace the market', by disadvantaging smaller competitors. This is especially evident where EU directives' specification criteria include components that have no bearing on the fitness for purpose or fitness for sale, but are intended merely to discriminate against and disadvantage one category of supplier to the market over another.

The key drivers of this corruption of purpose of the EU directive system are that the centralised bureaucracy pays disproportionate heed to large entities with organised lobbies, is generally not savvy enough to view markets holistically or savvy enough to adequately consider the full commercial and social impact of its regulation. These are particular problems when coupled with the EU's excessive zeal to centralise, regulate and control. In short, the EU legislative system and in particular the role of the European Commission renders it too vulnerable to manipulation by Big Business to be good for Europe's citizens. A consequence of the impact of what may be viewed as a legalised abuse of process has been seen by many Europeans as illegitimate and indeed unethical. As such it has stimulated much criticism of the EU itself. I would go further and say that in my opinion it has brought the European Commission into disrepute to the extent that it fuelled the call for Brexit and continues to drive anti-EU sentiment across the continent.

Acing the market by illegitimate/unethical abuse of large company power over a centralised bureaucracy is by no means restricted to the EU. Within the US, the Departments of Defence's (DoD) promulgation of the use of tungsten metal powder technology as the only 'non-toxic' metal in the US Army 'Green Ammunition' replacement program 1995 to 2005, and the US Department of Energy's (DoE) early restricted focus of public R&D funding on Powdered Activated Carbon technologies for mercury capture from power plant emissions (2000-2008) were quite probably attempts to 'ace the market' by commercial vested interest groups.

Lobbyists are not the only means by which organisations influence government and regulation. Large government bureaucracies and national industry trade bodies typically run light on industry-specific expertise and will subcontract technology evaluations and investigations for specific market applications to industry players to act as consultants to government or government quangos (quasi-governmental organisations). In doing so, they have to be mindful that the consultants they appoint act in a fair and unbiased way. Thus governments and quangos should avoid possibility of criticism for corporate manipulation and appoint consultants with zero conflict of interest. Where the appointed consulting organisation has a conflict of interest, i.e. they are a market player in the technology under evaluation, or one that competes with it, at the very least, any conflict of interest should be declared and there should be appropriate firewalls built into the consulting evaluation. For example, in the organisation with potential conflict of interest the actual personnel and their line management involved in the consulting projected should not be compromised by being active commercial players in the market, even if their organisation is. In this author's experience, within governmental and industry body organisations in UK, EU and US, ethical standards are weak in declaration of potential conflicts of interest and maintaining organisational firewalls, to the point where a single consultant might be appointed who has direct management of contracts posing a conflict of interest to the governmental project, yet does not declare them. The creation of an ethical firewall through the brain of the same person in such a circumstance is impossible, unless that consultant has a perfect multiple personality disorder. Would government departments be so naïve and would some consultants be so unethical? With regret the answer to both questions is an unsurprising 'Yes'.

The chief characteristics of 'acing the market' are:

- Reliant on a manipulatable or gullible centralised bureaucracy, usually via (a) political lobbying or (b) providing central government with biased technical input, portrayed as unbiased reporting.

- Enacted by larger market players (and their lobbyists), whose voice is disproportionately listened to by politicians and regulators.

- Aims to restrict competition via regulation or creating regulatory bias.

- Aims to restrict competition, if not to a single product, to a single technology option or product class, thereby barring potential substitutes offering superior performance via alternative technology.

- Aims to freeze the market condition thereby permanently locking in major players' advantage and creating a barrier to market disruption that fixes the market into a condition of rapidly aging 'Old Tech'.

All circumstances of illegitimately 'acing the market' run contrary to the public good. Governments have been lax in preventing their occurrence, largely because of the massive financial clout that lobbyists wield, and bring to bear on no more than several hundred politicians worldwide. Consider this. There are only 535 members of the US Congress, and 751 members of the EU parliament with only 28 EU Commissioners. Amongst these, there are no more than a few hundred key individuals with significant power, who can wield influence over economies comprising 50% of the world's GDP.

8.2.3 Defending and Assailing Markets

In a market in or approaching maturity, with little to distinguish their offers, the established market players compete primarily on price and thus vie for cost leadership with one another. These increased challenges to achieve cost leadership by management come at the time in the organisation's evolution when its jobs tend to become less attractive than career opportunities in rapidly growing and changing organisations. In vying for cost leadership, management quality can decline unless particular attention is paid by those responsible for HR. Usually the first thing closed down is research and development. In ceasing to look outward to the wider market for ideas and inspiration, and potentially new product and market developments, companies turn inward, focusing on maintaining own business, whilst keeping a weather eye on their closest-ranking competitors. This behaviour in maturity (or commercial old age) is equivalent to corporate dementia, with corporate atrophy paralleling that of the human condition. The organisation's ability to listen to its customers fails, it fails to see new innovations and their threat to their business until it's too late, and when the threat is perceived, the organisation's judgment is impaired and it does not make the logical, rational choice of action.

In seeking cost leadership the ethical market players execute such strategies as:

- Seek economies of scale, through merger and acquisition.

- Rationalise supplier networks.

- Optimise distribution arrangements for lowest cost to serve the end market.

- Form strategic alliances with companies offering related products, in a bid to stimulate market pull through co-offering synergistic products.

In seeking to maintain market share, unethical market players execute such strategies as:

- Raising structural barriers, through governmental and industry trade bodies' regulation on standards (acing the market). This may include seeking implementation of or increases to Customs and Excise tariffs or de-facto hidden tariffs, for example costs to comply with EU REACH registration.

- Having raised structural barriers, the residual market players will seek to form an informal or formal cartel.

- Raise the threat of retaliation.

- Lowers profitability in selective market sectors thereby making it less attractive to new market entrants – in other words poison pilling the market.

Essentially the actions of the unethical organisation in maturity are largely not focused on lowering its costs, but comparatively increasing costs for the established market competition or would be market entrants, or by reducing their potential rewards. With effective protectionist barriers raised, the unethical would 'circle the wagons' by forming an informal or formal cartel to stabilise or increase prices to the end customer.

Threatening the competition is a serious matter. What with and just how far do you go? I recall a time when I sold dyes for the plastic coloration market. By virtue of an accident of history, my company found itself to be the last manufacturer in the developed world of one of the only two dyes used to colour car tail lights red. Our principal competitor was a large German multinational, and their plant to make the dye in question had just been closed. As the product manager, I was happily seeing my product enquiries and sales climb steadily. I was already in the process of arranging a sales tour around Germany and the Low Countries, when I received a call from the large multinational requesting that I visit their head office. We neither bought from this company nor sold much to them. An ideal opportunity for cooperation, I thought. We could supply to them and then we'd still get some of the value-added of their market share whilst not stimulating them to look elsewhere, i.e. the Far East for supply.

On arriving at the swish offices of the German multinational housed in a glass-fronted tower block, I was shown to my potential client's offices. As I was ushered through his secretary's office to meet with the big man, my marketing senses ever tingling, I was scanning all around me for unguarded communications, indications of what they were up to and who was doing what ... Then I saw in the secretary's in tray upside down but unmistakeable, my quotes to a client in the Netherlands and my unopened samples to the same firm. Interesting, I thought, they have been busy boys. I was introduced to my opposite number in the multinational, Arnfried, a large imposing man, several years my senior with a splendid moustache. We shook hands warmly, going through the usual introduction niceties of exchanging cards and explaining what we did. Then I commenced my sales pitch. I could see from the look in his eyes that really he wasn't interested; he was just weighing me up. After my spiel he said he didn't think my product was of sufficient quality for them (it was in fact the highest quality and purity product on the market, and of course the sample he had was still unopened in the secretary's in tray) but he said he would consider my sales proposition to supply them as we stood to say our farewells. He walked me to the door of his office and placing his right hand firmly on my shoulder said to me, *"Peter, what you don't seem to understand..."* and whilst bringing the flat of his left hand to his chest continued quite firmly, *"this is our market and you've no place in it"*. He added, *"If you go on trying to steal our business it won't work out well for your little outfit"*. Now, I don't know if it's just me but I didn't take that as a real threat, only on the grounds that whatever proverbial club he thought he had to beat me with, in my eyes was no more than a balloon on a stick. I'm probably not the brightest penny in the pot and at that time I couldn't work out how a market of such size could be owned, at least not by an apparently reputable firm (yes, I was young and naïve in those days). And what could they do about it if I chose to dispute the issue in the marketplace? It puzzled me all the way back to the UK, and even as I packed to go to the US to seal a deal taking Arnfried's largest million dollar plus account for the tail light red from him, I still hadn't worked it out. But I eventually did when I got to America. Turned out that Arnie couldn't supply the tail light red anymore, but could offer a more expensive substitute and was trying to wean his biggest US customer onto that on the grounds that the old red dye was no longer available. Arnie was secretly frightened I'd screw up his 'no-longer-available' pitch. For him it was tough; with a good measure of input from our US agent I got the account and Arnie got early retirement shortly after.

In my experience people who make threats, be it personal or corporate are (a) usually more frightened of you than you are of them and (b) have self-esteem issues. There are times in the Anglo-Saxon language when the use of profanity is deemed acceptable to add the correct amount of emphasis to a point, so here goes (with apologies in advance to the sensitive at heart). Threatening anyone in business is a 'fucking stupid' thing to do, especially when you don't know them exceptionally well, and on all other occasions its extremely ill-advised. If the person or organisation threatened has an ounce of chutzpah, when forewarned by the threat they will be very likely motivated to get their retaliation in first.

Where a defender of a market in maturity sees a new market entrant, they can be minded to selectively lower market profitability. Take this example. A former multinational in the textile dye market, on seeing the first Indian dyes appearing in their 100%-controlled Middle Eastern market, selectively lowered its prices to cost at every account where the Indian competition was detected. This effectively poison pilled the business at that account. The multinational company's product manager deemed that the Indian competitor would eventually perceive there would be no profit in that market and withdraw, at which time the multinational would then increase their prices again. The Indian competitor was an astute man and perceived the market had been poison pilled. Consequently he sent free bulk samples out to the whole market and offered to match the multinational's cut prices, effectively calling the multinational's bluff. The multinational, seeing their bluff called and being faced with zero profit from the whole market, relented and restored normal pricing. Thus, the Indian competitor gained entry into the market and took a reasonable market share. In general, poison pilling markets is a poor strategy and one that can easily backfire on the larger market incumbent.

When entering a market in, or approaching maturity, the market usually has a finite size into which has grown an economically stable number of players, each with overcapacity. Were a new player to enter the market, without significant market growth, something would have to give. Thus a new entrant would have to heavily resource their planned entry to shove other players out, or buy a place at the table through merger or acquisition. To enter the market in such a way would inevitably need a motivation. The new entrant would have to perceive that they could through entry achieve extra value-added. It might be that they bring some synergy with other operations or added resources to re-tool and reinvigorate the player they have taken over. Thus far, there is nothing unethical in such a market entry strategy; however, once in, the new player, having been invigorated by the managed change challenges will usually be more motivated than most to make an impact and grow market share or improve profitability. They may even buy out other players in a bid to achieve economies of scale and reduce industry overcapacity, by buying out competitors, only to asset strip and close them.

But if you're unethical, what else could you do to take down your competition or remove their capacity? On one occasion I encountered, the market entrant, having purchased a major player in a niche market and knowing some dirt on their next closest competitor's environmental behaviour, made a call to the factory inspectorate. And 'hey-presto', the competitor was closed down. Was this unethical? It certainly was not criminal to report an offence. On another similar occasion the closest competitor's factory burned down (a serendipitous incident, I'm sure). Either way, the motivation of the new entrant will engender them toward an aggressive market stance, and such organisations, if fundamentally unethical, will be exceptionally motivated to justify their acquisition by seeking success not just by market share in terms of buying their competitors, but by buying business (see (5.1) The Problem with Selling).

Entrants into markets through merger or acquisition:

- Rationalise operations.

- Adopt an aggressive market presence.

- May seek to buy market share or buy-out overcapacity.

- May seek to eliminate competitors by any means allowed by their ethical standards.

- Exhibit a greater propensity to buy business via any means allowed by their ethical standards.

Disruptive innovation has been defined by Clayton M. Christensen in 1995[63] as an innovation that creates a new market and value network and eventually disrupts an existing market and value network, displacing established market leading firms, products and alliances. Disruptive innovations radically change the way markets work. They do not miraculously make new markets appear from nothing. The introduction of the telephone did not create the market to communicate over distance; it merely disrupted and eventually superseded the wire telegraph, as the introduction of the mobile phone has disrupted the landline telephone market. Thus most markets can be envisaged as behaving cyclically between phases of disruption, followed by rapid growth, which eventually slows into maturity, only for the mature market to become the subject of a new phase of disruption.

When seeking to enter a new market, disruptive innovation provides a route to overcome barriers, such as economies of scale. Thus you can have a dominant market player in photography, with huge cost leadership advantages in photo-reprographic chemicals such as Kodak being all but totally annihilated over two decades by the advent of digital imagery, and its capabilities offering new value added to consumers and substantively undercutting market costs of paper photoreproduction. Such an oversight on Kodak's part was largely down to seeing itself as a photographic company, yet the reality was with 12,000 employees out of 16,000 making chemicals for photography, it was a chemical company. Had Kodak viewed itself as a chemical imagery company it could have diversified into wider photo-reprographics, digital inks and even into the market for electronic display chemicals, all of which are now big business for its one-time Far Eastern competitors in Japan and Korea. This is a salutary lesson that illustrates the power of disruption as a means to enter markets and what can happen when an established player fails to deal with the new wave of disruption of a market place.

Disruption in itself is not unethical. It provides end users with additional value added and can reduce the costs of meeting existing demands. With appropriate innovation it can so effectively undercut existing market players as to render them commercially obsolete, or extinct. Now, if you're a market dinosaur and you see a disruptive mammal coming along and you know you're not going to be quick enough to evolve to meet the threat, what do you do? Ethical businesses would diversify and emulate the disruptive innovation, where possible. Even where disruptive innovation is covered by patent, there are ways and means, particularly under US law, to obtain effective clone patents, or combination patents, or subservient patents as a means to sidestep intellectual property protection barriers; not all these methods are legal or ethical. Such are the limitations of current practice in patent examination, I have even seen situations where technology from the 1930s, which may have passed from most up-to-date learning, has been re-patented in the last decade. The unethical would seek to use 'acing the market' strategies to raise barriers against the new innovation and where possible even try to eliminate their new rivals company by an aggressive market counter response including engaging with anti-competitive practices. Usually the last tactic they will try is simply emulating the market disruptor.

Where an establish market player meets disruption they will:

- Seek to overcome IP barriers protecting the disruptor.

- Seek to raise barriers against the disruptive innovation in its application or in its market launch.

- Seek to eliminate the competitor organisation, either by legitimate purchase or unethical means.

- Emulate the market disruptor by copycatting.

The rise and fall of Laker Airways' 'Skytrain' perhaps epitomises the processes involved where disruptive innovation meets an establish market that is aggressively defended by a heavyweight incumbent. In the 1970s, Freddie Laker was one of the first to offer 'no-frills' flights to New York. After years of battling with British regulators and the bigger established airlines, the first 'Skytrain' operated by Laker Airways flew from London's Gatwick airport to New York's JFK on September 26th 1977. The company was to go bust five years later.

Laker had correctly identified that the was a market for low-cost, 'no-frills' discounted airfares for transatlantic flights. At the time, the established major carriers ignored this market demand because they just couldn't service that sector at profitably due to their massive infrastructural costs. Laker's mistake in entering the market was that he was undercapitalised, and to meet slimmer margins he needed to fill capacity all-year round, and not just in peak holiday seasons. The major carriers, in sensing Laker's financial weakness, sought to stretch him as far as they could by placing pressure on regulators. Laker lacked the financial muscle to fight back in the courts. When Laker's cut-to-the-bone and asset-light business model began to come unstuck, he formulated a restructured business plan with the aid of aircraft makers McDonald Douglas (makers of the DC-10) and GE (makers of the DC-10's CF6 engine). BCal (British Caledonian), on discovering of the rescue package, wrote an open letter to other operators of the DC-10/CF6 in Europe saying that BCal, on behalf of all European operators, warned McDonnell Douglas and GE that in the event of the rescue for Laker being approved, none of these airlines would do business with those companies. As a consequence, the deal was scuppered and Laker's 'Skytrain' went under owing £270 million[64].

When Virgin Airways followed in Freddie Lakers' business model, it met the same type of competitor resistance from BA, but being forewarned by Laker's advice and being properly resourced, Richard Branson fought back and won[65]. Thanks to Sir Freddie Laker, the likes of Virgin, easyJet and even Ryanair were able to follow in his wake and meet less opposition. Even BCal were later acquired in 1987 by BA to form the basis of their low-cost no-frills market offer.

8.3 Mind the Gap

The market for cars is complex. Everyone wants a new car but not everyone can afford it. The market segment that can't or won't pay for a new car will pay for a slightly used car at lower prices, but that sub-prime market size is so disproportionately large relative to new car sales, that there are insufficient year-old used cars to fulfil demand. The car industry solves the problem by producing both new and second-hand cars. To produce the second-hand cars, they supply new cars to the rental market at knockdown prices and buy them back after one year or so and sell them on into the trade as second-hand cars appropriately priced. Thus, the car industry manages to meet demand from the secondary market, whilst not damaging its premium primary market. This ensures that all available gaps in the market are filled and the car makers sell more product.

Consider the marketing of premium-branded designer goods. The power of brand marketing places such goods at the top of many consumers' must-have lists. Even those who can't afford them desire them. Thus the overspill of what should have been niche premium-brand marketing has created an unfulfilled market gap. This unfulfilled demand in the sub-premium market should be unfulfillable owing to the copyright protection of the premium good, and of course because to fulfil that sub-market demand at affordable prices would tarnish the brand image of the premium good.

Markets behave organically, almost following Darwin's theories on natural selection in their mechanics. Where a gap exists, something will evolve to satisfy that demand. Now when it comes to dodgy designer brands, the image comes to mind of a Del Boy Trotter type, dressed in a sheepskin jacket and hawking his goods from the back of a Reliant Robin, and controlling his mini-empire from a council flat in Peckham. The truth is a world away. Fake goods are big business, big businesses are always large and well-financed and criminal big businesses are at least as well-organised as their legitimate counterparts.

I recall during one of my many visits to Hong Kong, I was taken on a tour of a textile factory in Kowloon. The factory, quite modern by any standards, was equipped with the most up-to-date Italian engineered embroidery machines. They were indeed a sight to behold working, churning out elaborate poster-sized silk embroideries of the type that are peddled to tourists, and reams upon reams of cap badges and clothing labels, most notably those of famous designer brands. Noting the reams of designer labels and knowing Hong Kong's reputation for 'copy-goods' I asked my host where the labels were destined for. My host wasn't fazed, and replied in a very matter-of-fact way, saying he didn't get involved in any illegalities with regard copyright, he made the labels for the companies who owned those brands, but then he smiled and said, and of course, to meet their exacting quality standards and lead-time needs, *"sometimes we have overruns"*. In one section of the factory, I noted the embroidered badges were being measured out, and different logos and other labels saying 'made in Italy', 'made in Germany' etc., were being portioned out into clear polythene sacks which then had a docket attached by tape. Periodically, trucks carrying 20 ft shipping containers would arrive in the factory's yard, a worker would check the container's ID, collect a bag of labels with the corresponding ID, and he would then open the container door, throw in the bag and close it again. The container would then leave the site. A few discreet questions later, and I discovered that the containers carried clothing and other apparel ware that were manufactured in Indonesia and the Philippines, where the workers then were paid 70 cents a day. The clothing, everything from T-shirts to designer leather goods were then sent to Hong Kong, combined with their labels and sent up into Guangdong for the labels to be sown on and the goods finished, by workers earning U$3 per day. It was explained to me that it was all a legitimate business really. The goods were routed from Hong Kong to Europe through Genoa, with the whole supply chain being managed by reputable Italian clothing merchants for and on behalf of major German clothing distribution chains.

If you have a business based on premium-branded goods, strategically it is a poor business decision to locate manufacturing into the developing world just to make a few extra bucks in the short term, because by doing so you lose product supply-chain security. If the sub-prime market grows to such a pitch that it overshadows your premium brand, ultimately you will damage it. Burberry is a typical example of a premium brand that grew downward into its sub-prime market, necessitating the company's 'brand reinvention' and turnaround in 2006[66]. Quite clearly premium brand defence via copyright enforcement needs to be pursued. However, why do purveyors of premium brands allow their advertising and promotion to spill over such that it stimulates or in some cases overstimulates sub-prime demand? If you create a market demand you can't fulfil, then someone else will. Consider the plight of the owners of premium designer goods brands. They are probably making less money on their prime sales than they could if they had control of their sub-prime market. But perhaps they do indirectly control their sub-prime markets?

9. Business Intelligence and Espionage

9.1 Business Intelligence

Marketing is to business what military intelligence is to warfare. As typified by the approach of Reinhard Gehlen (Hitler's spymaster and one of the founding fathers of the modern CIA and the German BND (Bundesnachrichtendienst / Federal Intelligence Service)), the gathering and of *"all-encompassing knowledge"* combined with its analysis is the cornerstone of intelligence. To that end, marketing professionals use numerous methods of data gathering: customer interviews, customer surveys, competitor surveys, market reports, filed company accounts, technology journals and reviews, press reports, economic studies, academic text books... The list is endless, and virtually everything gatherable is out there within the public domain. Well, almost everything, let's say 99% of it. All companies will hold certain information confidential and secret. This may include business plans, the products of research, designs and drawings, commercial contracts and communications, its management accounts, privileged legal documents, communications, personnel records and its own marketing reports. These secrets are the 1% or so of materials that are the 'intellectual property' of others that the marketing manager of an adversarial organisation might like to get hold of, but would be prohibited to access by ethical means.

In his autobiography, Gehlen pays tribute to Sun Tzu's 5th-century BCE treatise on the *The Art of War* for its depiction of the need for intelligence and the manners of it. Though a version of this work has been adapted for the modern executive world by Donald Krause[67],not all of Sun Tzu's wisdom translates into the modern executive environment. However admirable, tossing dead horses into the enemy's water supply was back in the 5th century BCE, I think that poisoning the competitor's office water cooler is taking unethical conduct way too far. But other aspects of modern-day corporate intelligence have their parallels in the old narratives with regard to 'internal intelligence', 'counter intelligence' (including the spreading of misinformation)', 'scouts and explorers', 'treachery', and 'espionage'.

When it comes to paralleling modern commercial practice with war we have similar regulation and boundaries regarding intelligence or, as we like to call it, 'marketing'. With regards to scouting and exploring the lay of the land, all these aspects are in the ethical realm of the marketing manager in the 99% of publicly available data. Internal intelligence is also an aspect of marketing, as in order to make meaningful commercial plans one needs a realistic appraisal of one's organisation's own internal capabilities. Counter intelligence has two aspects, (1) internal security to prevent and detect treachery and espionage directed from within and without the organisation, and (2) misinformation to misdirect or distract the attentions of competitors from the organisation's real intentions, both of which are or usually conductible within the full remit of a legally ethical organisation. On the other hand, treachery and espionage are well outside the realms of ethical conduct and in most cases way into the realm of criminal conduct, and comprise that 1% of data that the truly ethical should not go in search of.

9.2 Industrial Espionage

In modern times, industrial espionage largely takes two forms: theft of commercial secrets (with or without the aid of treachery) and industrial sabotage.

9.2.1 Theft of Commercial and Industrial Secrets

Industrial espionage or commercial espionage has a long history, with notable examples being Francois Xavier's work *d'Entrecolles* published in 1712, which disclosed Chinese trade secrets for the manufacture of fine porcelain china, and even earlier when two Christian monks smuggled silkworms and carried the secret of silk making out of China to the Byzantine empire in the reign of Justinian I, in the 6th century. So how ironic it is that China, which has given so much to the world in the form of technologic art (i.e. learned teaching), is now considered to be the world's greatest illicit acquirer of the same. Consider, just 50 years ago, China was largely an agriculturally based third-world economy. Today, with a population exceeding 1.3 billion, it's a world power if not a superpower, with a US$30 billion trading surplus with the US. It holds US$1 trillion plus in US treasury debt, produces a million more cars per annum than the US and has outpaced the US in domestic PC sales. To quote Hannas and Mulvenon's thesis[68] on 'Chinese industrial Espionage':

"One decade ago we could not have believed it ourselves. Like most Americans, we were aware of China's economic progress and of complaints that this progress relied in part on prior Western art [knowledge]. So what? This is the globalized twenty-first century. We patent products, they build them and pay royalties, the world moves on. Let the music industry worry about pirated CDs.

The point is that China was not – and is not – paying, and the "piracy" issue barely scratches the surface. Indeed, one could argue that our obsession with counterfeiting distracts us from the real threat from China, namely its ability to latch onto high technology created abroad, and apply it to real products – without compensating its owners.

This brings us to the heart of the matter; while giving due credit to the Chinese people for their ability to produce, China could not have engineered this transformation, nor sustained its progress today, without cheap and unrestricted access to other countries' technology."

Thus China stands accused of rampant theft of the West's industrial intellectual property. But is this for real? Most certainly the UK government takes it seriously with some estimates putting the cost of espionage to UK companies in excess of £30 billion per annum. However, that is losses due to all sources and not just China. And it should not be ignored that some contend that the US has its own government-sponsored cyber economic spying program that has been running since the 1970s.

9.2.2 Sabotage

Industrial sabotage takes two forms. One arises from industrial grievance within the firm in industrial conflict where worker protests become manifest as workplace sabotage; as such it should be regarded as a sub-issue of industrial relations. Though little studied there is valid literature on this rare topic worthy of note in passing such as that by Farhad Analoui of the University of Bradford.[69] Our principal concern is industrial sabotage originating externally to the organisation, specifically by commercial competitors. On this subject, due to its covert characteristics and taboo nature, there is scant discussion in management literature. Yet in my experience, it does happen, and more frequently than you might anticipate. I do not concern myself with issues of counter marketing, such as opposing a competitor's marketing promotions or product launches by counter marketing or misinformation, all of which might be considered ethical, at least by a legally ethical organisation. I define sabotage as an act of unethical or unlawful destruction of property, or unlawful obstruction by one party of another party or organisation pursuing its rightful and lawful activities.

I have encountered several examples of extraneous physical and economic sabotage. I shall recount one of the most memorable ones, that sticks in my mind for its blatancy and brazenness. In my capacity as a consultant working for a principal, I had been contracted to design and develop a new chemical process. My principal had made an agreement with a large US engineering firm in relation to the testing of the process in the firm's lab, ostensibly with a view to the engineering firm purchasing or licensing the process. I arrived with a colleague and together with the engineering firm's chief R&D scientist commenced the tests, which were scheduled to run for a week. The lab was windowless and the site, a featureless typical engineering plant, had scant canteen facilities for lunch. We had to bring in sandwiches, which we could eat in a windowless meeting room right next to the toilet. For coffee, there was a help-yourself bar in the sales department. The sales department, which was about the size of a tennis court, at least had windows. It was all open-plan, with individual desks being partitioned off by chest-high panelling and arranged around a central corridor. In the middle, on one long wall near the entry from the plant, was the coffee bar. The site had no particular security, save for a man on the main gate; we weren't even required to wear a visitor's tag, and I could walk freely around. My host hadn't introduced me to any of the members of the commercial team, just those whom we were working with in the lab. So throughout the week, on several occasions per day I was a regular visitor to the coffee bar and was almost part of the sales department's landscape. Nobody knew who I was; they just believed that I worked at the plant. The lab testing had gone particularly well, so well that the firm's chief R&D scientist was amazed and admitted that the technology was way ahead of anything they had by several orders of magnitude. My colleague and I thought there were real prospects that the technology might get commercialised very rapidly and I admit

I was beginning to get a little excited. It was then I got a tap on my shoulder and a little bird said. *"They're never going to buy your process, you know."* With my forehead now furrowed and one eyebrow raise I said, *"What?"*. *"They're never going to buy your process, just take a walk down to sales,"* the bird said. So I toddled off to sales to get a coffee. Arriving in sales, everything seemed normal and I helped myself to the usual, a large white with one sugar. On stirring my drink and turning around I noticed a small huddle in the middle of the corridor in the partitioning. I was less than 10 feet away and there were three individuals talking about our process. They had heard about the test results and were concerned as it was far superior by miles to the one they had introduced to the market less than a year back. The individuals, one of whom was apparently a sales manager, the other a product manager and the third a project engineer, seemingly had no concept or intention of launching our process as a new improved technology. Their only concern was, 'Okay, we have a threat, now how do we kill it'. And in the middle of an open-plan office without consideration of any commercial or legal implications with a major security breach standing just 10 feet away, they discussed ways in which they could lure my principal into a contract which would result in an un-ending development project, to keep them out of approaching the market themselves and undermining the engineering firm's existing product. It must be a truly rare occasion that when a party becomes the subject of an espionage plot by a competitor, it gets to view the actuality of the plotting as a 'fly-on-the-wall', but this was one such occasion. I just wished I'd had a tape recoder or modern phone with me at the time.

Naturally I immediately alerted my principals as to the firm's ill-intent and I assume they took some contractual precautions because against my better judgement but under a US-DoE grant-funded program, they agreed to undertake scale-up trials with the same firm, using our process as an environmental treatment to be used on a third party's plant. My principals naïvely assumed that as it was a DoE-funded program that it would be properly run and independently supervised. I oversaw the scale-up trials for my principal, but guess who was appointed overall project manager? None other than the project engineer from the duplicitous firm that I had encountered plotting in the sales department. The scale-up trials went exceedingly well considering, with early positive results, shocking the project engineer. We had to hit an 80% efficiency target and we'd have beaten the industry's best, and we were well on our way to that target. That's when we hit problems. The third party had agreed a protocol to maintain continuous uniform operations, while we co-dosed our treatment process. The third party breached the agreed protocol, changing its raw materials without notice, and in doing so producing a much harder to treat waste – yet our process dealt with it. Then the project manager tried to halt the trial, claiming it was compromising the operation of the third party's process. With the aid of his own subordinate test engineer I proved that the project manager's assertions were wrong. The tests were then resumed and apparently the project engineer sent his subordinate back to base in disgrace, so short-handed we pressed on. Then there was an attempt to physically sabotage our addition system. Apparently, a half-inch ball valve operated via a horizontal lever was moved into the closed position, nearly causing a reagent addition pump to catastrophically fail. With the pump screaming it was caught just the nick of time by my colleague. The closing of the lever was a difficult thing to do by accident as it was in a taped-off area of the plant and the lever was secured in the open position by a nylon security tie. We overcame the problem with just a few percent to go to break the target and with a further two days of the trial yet to run, and then the project manager call a halt to the trial. My colleague and I just looked at each other dumbfounded, as there was nothing we could do to overrule him. The results were due to be reported to the DoE a couple of weeks later by our not-so-friendly project manager. On receiving a copy of the draft presentation to be made to the DoE by the project manager, the results were not those obtained and of course I had copies of all the raw data. I had to forcefully demand an amendment to his presentation. The presentation was corrected, with the false data taken out. However, the project manager didn't declare the full positive results that we obtained or explain the adversarial conditions against which they were gained. Personally I put much of the blame for the overall fiasco with the DoE for its lack of forethought in ceding control of the project to a party with a clear vested interest to protect their own established business, and, worse still, use exactly the same personnel, who actively promoted that established business, as DoE rapporteurs.

9.3 Treachery

It's sad that treachery exists, but it does in the real world, and it's a sad day indeed when you can't trust those your company has a right to expect a fiduciary duty from, especially from allegedly competent professionals. It's one of the uglier facets of business life. The key mover must be a facilitator who can induce the malfeasance of a paid employee or a contractually or professional bound associate to the company thus:

- Induce another's employees to break their fiduciary duties to their employer by betraying company secrets.

- Induce customer's employees to break their fiduciary duties to their employer by selling influence or access (see: The Problem with Selling (5.1) and Corrupt Buyers (5.2.2)).

- Induce another's associates bound by fiduciary duty, i.e., its lawyers, accountant, bankers or consultants to sell company secrets or influence.

Some 20 years ago, I took charge of the front-end European sales distribution unit based in Manchester for an Indian colorants manufacturer. Our business unit was capitalised with £500,000 in cash from our parent company and we were growing very rapidly. To fuel our growth, our group finance director asked that we obtain local overdraft facilities for a further £500,000, and I was requested to prepare a comprehensive business plan for submission to the bank. I duly prepared the plan, of which I am proud, as apart from accurately laying out the landscape and economics of the market, it predicted the development and contractions of the main players and the market, and consequences thereof over the next ten years. Our local bank was the local subsidiary of our parent company's bank in India. My finance director, himself a respected retired banker of impeccable credentials, prepared the request documents and along with my plan handed it into our local branch personally. Over a month later and we still had not heard anything from the bank. Anticipating they were perhaps slow for cultural reasons, as in India things tend to take their own pace, I was not unduly alarmed. That was until I had dinner with Nic, an old friend in the same trade. He was a London-based Indian trader in dyestuffs, like his father before him a very well-known and well-regarded personality. We'd met up for a curry and a night of drink and banter, mostly social but some business, with lots of chat and industry gossip. During the course of the evening Nic asked, *"What's your turnover?"* Like everyone in the trade I responded, not lying but not giving the accurate figures. After all, he could check them out down at Companies House in a year's time. Nic then proceeded to tell me what my turnover and my profit margin actually were to the pound. He then recited back to me parts of my business plan, a plan that had only ever been in the hands and sight of two people in my own company, one being me and the other my FD. Trying to not show surprise, I said, *"So, you've seen my business plan. What did you think?"* *"It's okay,"* he replied. *"How did you get hold of it?"* I queried. Nic replied, *"Oh, I was shown it by Mr B. He got it from your bank."* And he added, *"He has high-level contacts there and has access to anything he wants. Oh, and by the way, that overdraft you're after, you're not going to get it. B has made sure of that."* Well, that explained the abnormal delay in the overdraft request, and confirmed my company's confidential secrets had found their way out of my bank and into a Huddersfield curry house, apparently by being sold to a competitor by my own banker who had further sold his own influence to block my business dealings. The next day, first thing, I notified my FD as to what had transpired the night before. I then took a copy of my plan around to my personal bank, Barclays in Manchester. On behalf of my company, I filed a request for a facility for a £500,000 overdraft. The next day two business bankers from Barclays arrived at our offices to assess our operation and they happily agreed our facilities, subject to us moving our banking over to them. The whole process was concluded within 48 hours. And the company still banks with them to this day. And the rub is, we hardly every used the overdraft.

Mr B was of course quite a feature in our trade. He had a habit of knowing things, and he was also an adept spinner of misinformation and downright lies, especially to large European companies, whose buyers rarely left their offices. I met a trader who had very early dealings with him. He had a largish trading company, bought goods from B and then either formulated them into products or simply re-sold them on to his principal client, a larger corporation where he had some personal contacts. B apparently wanted to cut him out to sell direct but he didn't know who the end customer was. Somehow he got the name of the end client and the contact. Mr B's only problem was he liked to brag to his mates about his exploits, his business prowess, acumen and guile, and that's how Nic got to know of my banking issue. It's also how the trader came to know that B used to visit his company's industrial estate at night and remove their office waste sacks from the commercial waste dumpster outside their premises.

It wasn't to be the last time I'd run across Mr B. In pursuit of my company's business, I'd regularly make sales tours, visiting clients and potential clients located on the near continent. I'd regularly do a week-long tour by car, crossing from Hull via the ferry and run a circuit from the Benelux countries down the Rhine valley as far as Basle, ending by visiting clients in northern France, then driving north again on the Saturday to Zeebrugge and returning to the UK via ferry overnight. As I was trained with all commercial activities, I compiled a detailed visit report on who I'd seen, what I'd found out and what business prospects there were, and of course what quotations I'd given out. This report went to my superiors at head office (HO) in Mumbai, at that time via fax. About two weeks after one such trip, I had feedback from my clients that a close, Indian-based competitor had visited every one of the accounts I had visited on my last tour. Though comparatively new to the market, they knew exactly what business was already there and offered quotations exactly 20 cents per kilogram lower relative to the varied quotations I had left at each account. Were it not for the lower quality of their product in comparison to our own, we'd potentially have lost a lot of business. There was obviously a leak somewhere and I could vouch for my end because I personally was the only person in Europe to have a legitimate copy of my visit report. I advised HO and they said they'd look into the matter but they trusted their staff and didn't think they had a problem. Some months later I visited our Mumbai HO personally and they still hadn't found the source of the leak. When later discussing some details at one particular account I referred my director to a prior visit report I'd made. Strangely, he said he hadn't seen it let alone read it. He called his secretary to bring in my communications file. Now it's almost standard practice in any sales department that they will have a physical paper file for all agents, clients and even competitors, basically anyone they are interested in or had communicated with. Even in this computer-driven world with a lot of data stored in electronic format, each file usually comprises a Manila folder wherein all communications are

169

physically stored in date order with the newest communication being on top. The files housed alphabetically in four-drawer filing cabinets. The secretary returned with my file, and to the amazement of all of us it was virtually empty. On detailed scrutiny, the files of other key agents were also somewhat light, and their businesses also overlapped with the key commercial area where we were having problems with the same Indian-based competitor. It seems our mole, not wanting to be seen acting untoward by visiting the photocopier too often, was actually taking original documents home with him. His error was, where he should have copied them and returned the original, he didn't and thereby advertised his turpitude. In some cases the mole was so keen he'd lift documents hot from the fax machine before those they were intended for had time to read them. The matter was addressed on that occasion but the basic problem never fully went away, commercial data security issues forever plagued the company. Somehow we learned to live with it and thrived, but I never again filed a formal written sales report.

From my wider business contacts in India, I actually discovered that Mr B had his very own spy network. In virtually every major Indian company in our sector he had a mole to whom he paid a retainer of a staggering US$100–200 per month. Now at that time in India in our business sector, that would equate to 10 to 20% on top of a legitimate middle-manager's salary. The stooges were located in key sales and technical departments, such that Mr B could get access to any process he desired and he was usually advised within 24 hours of any key parcel of business that was available, along with his competitor's quotes. Where he was successful in intercepting profitable business using the stolen information, which could net him several tens of thousands to hundreds of thousands of dollars in profit on a single transaction, he paid a performance bonus. Where he found the stolen data was not directly exploitable by him, he'd sell it on to someone who could exploit it. And it was just from such an individual that I came to learn of Mr B's network. Mr B had a particular relationship with our closest competitor and it was he who was supplying them with my sales reports. The principal problem with India is that compared to the rest of the world, in most sectors salaries are pathetically poor and an extra US$200 a month tax-free coming in at that time bought a lot of happiness.

9.4 Prevention is Better Than Cure

The saying 'all's fair in love and war' might be assumed to have come from some noted play or bardic verse of antiquity. Some might take this saying as a statement of long standing that in war and love there are no rules and anything goes. But clearly, that's not the case. The saying originated in the early 20th century, the bloodiest in human history. All is definitely not fair in either love or war. In the modern era, due to its propensity for devastating impact on society, war is governed by many international laws, namely, Geneva Conventions of 1864, 1906, 1929; Hague Convention of 1899 and 1907; Geneva Convention on Geneva Protocol to Hague Conventions of 1925, 1928, 1975, 1993, over and above civil laws pertain to violent crime, destruction and breaches of human rights. Even in ancient times, warfare had codes of conduct, and so did business. Regarding the less savoury aspects of business intelligence – espionage, sabotage and treachery – these have always been punishable by statute. In modern times the punishments for various breaches will depend upon the nation and culture, expressing itself as local custom and practice. For example a conviction for industrial espionage in the US might land you two to three years inside plus a fine, in Switzerland the same offence would likely get you double that. Bribing a government official in the US can get you up to 15 years inside plus a fine. In China, the same offence can get you shot.

Given the variance in penalties worldwide, any international businessman should have due cognizance of what the consequences are of what is not to be done and of those countries where, if what should not be done, was done. Now that's fairly clear for the legally ethical company, if they stick to the right side of the law codes, there is a clear legally defined line as to what's doable and what's not. So, everyone knows where they stand – right! Except that's not the case, especially in Europe. As of June 8, 2016, the EC Directive 2016/943[70] on the protection of undisclosed know-how and business information (trade secrets) against their unlawful acquisition, use and disclosure, was issued. It defines unlawful acquisition, use and disclosure as: *"An unlawful acquisition will occur if the alleged infringer accesses or copies without authorisation, bribes, steals, breaches or induces to breach a confidentiality agreement and/or engages in 'any other conduct which, under the circumstances, is considered contrary to honest commercial practices'."* Honesty is a far bigger concept than legality. Thus a legally ethically compliant company in any Anglo-Saxon jurisdiction faces a double whammy when operating in a European jurisdiction under Romanic law of being not just obligated to do business *'in good faith'* but in matters relating to the intellectual property of others, hasn't to behave in a manner that might be construed as *'contrary to honest commercial practice'*. Such legislation is not without precedent. Long ago within the bounds of the City of London, there was an ethical concept backed by common-law precedent, that a gentleman's word was his bond. Though, to quote Lord Sugar, this *"is now no longer the case"*, an occurrence attributable to corporations favouring *'legal ethics'* over *'true ethics'*. The new EU directive, applicable within English and Welsh law, now reinstates that principle of *'honest commercial practice'* in law, at least in matters of intellectual property. The only true defence for a company not wishing to become embroiled in conflict arising from a misunderstanding as to what honest commercial practices are, is for a legally ethical company to become a truly ethical company. However, in the absence of the creation of an ethical utopia overnight, for the organisation that does not wish to be preyed upon by the less scrupulous, to quote the old Arabic proverb *'trust in Allah, but tie up your camel'*, i.e. expect the best behaviour of others, but plan for the worst. In planning for the worst, strategies for prevention of espionage should include:

Protect Information:

- Sensitive documents should be marked 'Strictly Private and Confidential' or 'Secret', and their circulation restricted.

- Operate a nightly 'clean desk' policy.

- Wipe whiteboards and working paper poster boards daily. Better still use electronic equivalents.

- Secure paper documents and ensure digital security of e-documents, with system firewalls, PC-passwords and restriction of physical access.

- Never allow unhindered access into sensitive areas, i.e. the sales and marketing departments, or research and development.

- All documents for disposal must be shredded or burned on site.

- All old PCs for disposal must have the hard drives retained – or the hard drives must be physically destroyed.

- For projects of high risk, have offices routinely swept for bugs.

- Never allow modern mobile phones or cameras into sensitive zones.

- Restrict the use of laptops and the capability to transfer sensitive data from secure zones.

- Entertain site visitors in dedicated areas away from sensitive zones.

Human resources:

- Train staff on the realities of espionage and prevention measures.

- Recruit the 'right people', i.e. avoid those with a predisposition to poor ethical conduct.

- Monitor those members of staff who might be vulnerable to subversion, or better get rid of those you can't trust.

- Avoid reliance on a single person of trust in any business-critical corporate function.

- Screen all personnel who work in sensitive zones, even the cleaners.

Business Strategy:

- Stay away from organisations/individuals with a poor reputation or aggressive business tactics.

- Strive to be a truly ethical organisation. Legalistic thinking isn't enough to stay on the right side of the law anymore.

- Expect the best but plan for the worst.

10. Let's be Careful Out There

It is a sad fact of life that amongst the spectrum of peoples in the world there is a fair slice of human kind with darker souls than most and deficient in the more noble features of humanity. They are evenly spread across the globe and come in every size, shape and form. Though a minority, they are sufficient in number to pervade every aspect of life, such that on our journey through it, encountering such individuals is inevitable. Even as I sit to type this text I am diverted by a telephone call. It was someone from a call centre in India claiming to be from BT, who informed me that as my computer is infected with viruses they are going to cut my internet connection unless I purchase antivirus software from them. This was a new one; last week they claimed to be from Microsoft and I'll swear it was the same 'boiler room' outfit from Bangalore. Calling the guy's bluff, I ask him how many people has he conned today, he laughed and calmly replied, "*In this callcentre, from Britain, about 2,000 a day*". Each is probably hit for £100 or more, with the elderly being the most preyed upon. Not many weeks earlier I received a letter from a 'trademark publishing journal' in Belgium, saying that they had noticed I had a trademark application renewed and I was required to publish the fact in their journal to guarantee its validity, and "*by the way, for your convenience we enclose our invoice for several hundred euros.*" You don't have to leave the comfort of your own home to be mugged these days; they do it down the phone lines and internet instead. Just today October 18, 2016, the BBC has reported that online cybercrime is costing the UK £10.9 billion a year or £210 per adult. In the real world of business and commerce where the stakes are higher and the parcels of cash transacted so much greater, the sharks are bigger and sometimes much nastier. The risks from theft, fraud and other unethical skulduggery are 'real' and sometimes 'existential threats', and it's a '*Dirty Business*' having to deal with and counter them, but almost everyone has to do it at some point in their career.

The largest companies have organised support infrastructure for most eventualities. They have established systems, up-to-date training, legal departments who dot the 'i's' and cross the 't's' as and when needed, and have sufficiently deep pockets to pay for them. They have established international representation and are usually wired into trade associations and governments. In comparison, the Small to Medium sized Enterprise (SME) has squat. If you're a small player and you get into trouble by becoming the victim of criminal and unethical practice out there in the big wide world, the UK government really doesn't want to be bothered. The best they'll do is provide you with a lawyer's telephone number and a loan for a ticket home. These days from government, even tea and sympathy are thin on the ground. Oh, and don't expect any business advice from government, even if proffered; it tends to be somewhat 'non-practitioner based'.

It stands to reason that everyone needs support from time to time, whatever their size of enterprise. To meet that requirement you need a support infrastructure. If you're only a one-man band or an SME, you have to build, reinforce and maintain your very own. It starts at home with family and friends. When you're deep in the doo-doo, you'll find out who your real friends are. Build professional and business networks in institutions such as your local Chamber of Commerce; value and aid them. Hopefully, again when you're up to your eyes in it, the goodwill you've sown, you'll reap and that's where you'll find expertise and aid in your time of need, and most of it offered freely. Treasure and value them all. They are your safety net when everything about you fails. And above all, be careful out there…

* * *

11. References

[1] Cialdini R.H., Petrova P.K. and Goldstein, N.J., 'The Hidden Costs of Organizational Dishonesty', *MIT Sloan Management Review* (15 April 2004).

[2] Lewis D.E., 'Corporate Trust a Matter of Opinion', *Boston Globe*, Sunday, p. G2 (23 Nov. 2003).

[3] Bucy P.H., Formby E.P., Raspanti M.S. and Rooney K.E., *'Why Do They Do It?:* The Motives, Mores, and Character of White Collar Criminals', *St. John's Law Review* Iss 2 and Volume 82, Number 2 Article 1 January 2012.

[4] Parry W., 'How to Spot Psychopaths: Speech Patterns Give Them Away', Live Science – *Health* (20 Oct. 2011).

[5] Chamorro-Premuzic T., *'The Dark Side of Charisma'*, The Harvard Business Review (16 Nov. 2012).

[6] Lipman V., 'The Disturbing Link Between Psychopathy and Leadership', *Forbes Magazine* (25 April 2013).

[7] Dutton K., *'The Wisdom of Psychopaths: What Saints, Spies, and Serial Killers Can Teach Us About Success'*, Scientific American / Farrar, Straus and Giroux (2012).

[8] Pearlman J., '1 in 5 CEOs are psychopaths, Australian study finds', *The Daily Telegraph* (13 Sep. 2016).

[9] Boddy C., Ladyshewsky R.K., Galvin P.G., 'Leaders without ethics in global business: corporate psychopaths', *Journal of Public Affairs* vol.10 (June 2010), 121–138.

[10] Mahmut, M., Homewood, J., Stevenson, R., 'The characteristics of non-criminals with high psychopathy traits: Are they similar to criminal psychopaths?', *Journal of Research in Personality,* (2008) 42 (3), 679–692.

[11] Soltes, E., 'Why They Do It – Inside the Mind of the White-Collar Criminal', *Public Affairs* (2016).

[12] Mintzberg H., *'Structure in Fives: Designing Effective Organizations'*, Prentice Hall International (1992).

[13] Stadler C. and Dyer D., 'Why Good Leaders Don't Need Charisma', *MIT Sloan Management Review* (19 March 2013).

[14] http://www.transparency.org/cpi2015

[15] http://www.transparencyinternational.com

16 Kar D. and Curcio K., 'Illicit Financial Flows from Developing Countries: 2000–2009 Update with a Focus on Asia', Global Financial Integrity, A Program of the Center for International Policy, Washington D.C. (2009).

17 The United States Department of Justice. 'Fraud Section Year in Review' (2015).

18 Milne R., 'Telia to cop $1.4bn fine over corruption in Uzbekistan', *Financial Times* (15 September 2016).

19 Estrel M. and Crawford D., 'Siemens to Pay Huge Fine in Bribery Inquiry', *The Wall Street Journal* (15 December 2008).

20 Press Association. 'Fifa opens corruption case against Sepp Blatter and Jérôme Valcke', *The Guardian* (6 September 2016).

21 Milliet-Einbinder M., 'Writing off tax deductibility', *OECD Observer* No 220 (April 2000).

22 Carter Dougherty, 'Germany takes aim at corporate corruption', *International Herald Tribune* – Business (14 February 2007).

23 Bloomberg News. *'Germany where bribery is tax deductible'* (7 August 1995).

24 Millar, J., 'Swiss government: Fines bribes should no longer be tax-deductible', Reuters - Zurich, (18 December 2015).

25 Mulcahy S., *'Money, Politics, Power: Corruption Risks in Europe', National* Integrity System (6 June 2012).

26 Current law across the EU from April 18, 2016. Directive 2014/24/EU on public procurement, Directive 2014/25/EU on procurement by entities operating in the water, energy, transport and postal services sectors, Directive 2014/23/EU on the award of concession contracts.

27 Babiak P. and Hare R.D., *'Snakes in Suits: When Psychopaths Go to Work'*, Harper Collins (7 June 2007).

28 Neff, T.J., Citrin, J.M. and Prown, P.B., *'Lessons from the Top: The Search for America's Best Business Leaders'*, Bantam Doubleday Dell Publishing Group (2000).

29 Miracle G.E., 'Product Characteristics and Marketing Strategy', *Journal of Marketing,* 29 (1965), 18–24.

30 Mayr W., 'The Mafia's Deadly Garbage – Italy's Growing Toxic Waste Scandal', *Der Spiegel* (16 January 2014).

31 Hall J., 'The Mafia mobsters bring Italy's economy to its knees by

infiltrating each business and public body in the south... and taking a cut from EVERY deal', *The Mail* (23 September 2015).

[32] Porter M.E., *'Competitive Strategy – Techniques for Analyzing Industries and Competitors'*, The Free Press 1980

[33] NB: European Union agency law (COUNCIL DIRECTIVE 86/653/EEC of 18 December 1986 on the coordination of the laws of the Member State relating to self-employed commercial agents) prevails within the EU, wherein the 'non-contract out-able of' aspect of the directive renders the prevailing law governing any sales agency to be the national law in the country in which the agency is enacted. Thus for an agency for a UK company conducted in Germany, German law is applicable. Under Germany law, sales commissions are due when the formal order is taken and payable to the agent even if the goods and not delivered and may be due even if the order otherwise falls through.

[34] Indian law specifically defines 64 industries as hazardous and since 1984 it has been a criminal offence to employ children under the age of 15 in hazardous industries.

[35] Asariotis R., Benamara H., Premti A., and Lavelle J., 'Maritime Piracy: An Overview of Trends, Costs and Trade-Related Implications', UNCTAD, 1 (2014).

[36] Sandle P. and Ed. Char P., 'Cyber crime costs global economy $445 billion a year: report', Reuters, TECHNOLOGY NEWS (9 June 2014).

[37] 'Annual Fraud Indicator 2016', PKF Accountants and Business Advisors, PKF Littlejohn LLP (May 2016).

[38] Aggarwal V., 'India the most targeted country for data breaches', *The Hindu - Business Line* (July 27, 2016).

[39] Sadgrove K., 'The Complete guide to business Risk management', Routledge (2016).

[40] Merlin Scott Associates Limited, Dunselma Castle, Strone, Dunoon, Argyll, PA23 8RU, Scotland http://www.merlinscottassociates.co.uk

[41] http://www.solicitorstribunal.org.uk/search/JudgementSearch.aspx

[42] The European Commission for the Efficiency of Justice, 'European Judicial Systems – Efficiency and quality of Justice', Edition 2014 (2012 data), CEPEJ Studies Nº20 (2014).

[43] Eyal Benvenisti E. and Downs G.W., 'National Courts, Domestic Democracy, and the Evolution of International Law', *The European*

Journal of International Law (EJIL), Vol. 20 No. 1 (2009), 59–72.

[44] Mackaay E., 'Good faith in Civil Law Systems', Centre interuniversitaire de recherché en analysis des organisations, Montreal (2011).

[45] Ramseyer, J.M., and Rasmusen, E.B., 'Comparative Litigation Rates', Harvard Law School Discussion Paper No.681 (November 2010).

[46] McCorquodale, R., McNamara, L., Kupelyants, H. and del Rio, J., 'Factors Influencing International Litigants', Decisions to Bring Commercial Claims to the London Based Courts', Eva Lein, Ministry of Justice, British Institute of International and Comparative Law (2015).

[47] 'Tort Liability Costs for Small Businesses,' U.S. Chamber Institute for Legal Reform (July 2010).

[48] 'How Many Lawsuits are There in the U.S. & What are They For? An Amazing Overview', www.SixWise.com / http://www.sixwise.com/newsletters/06/10/05/how-many-lawsuits-are-there-in-the-us--amp-what-are-they-for-an-amazing-overview.htm

[49] Brian Cave LLP, 'Enforcement of US Court Judgments in England', A broader Perspective Bulletin (August 2014).

[50] Zeynalova Y., *'The Law on Recognition and Enforcement of Foreign Judgments: Is It Broken and How Do We Fix It?'*, Berkeley Journal of International Law, Vol 31 Issue 1, Article 4 (2013).

[51] Perkins A., 'Blair's No Thinker – Haskins', *The Guardian* (8 February 2002).

[52] http://www.LCIA.org

[53] Friedland P. and Mistelis L., '2015 International Arbitration Survey: Improvements and Innovations in International Arbitration', Case & White, Queen Mary University of London and School of International Arbitration, http://www.arbitration.qmul.ac.uk/docs/164761.pdf

[54] https://wallethub.com/edu/states-where-identity-theft-and-fraud-are-worst/17549

[55] Jobber D. and Ellis-Chadwick F., *'Principles and Practice of Marketing'*, McGraw-Hill, 7th Ed 2013, 8th Ed (2016).

[56] Kotler P. and Heller K.L., *'Marketing Management'*, Prentice-Hall, 14th Ed. (2012).

[57] Porter M.E., *'The Competitive Strategy: Techniques for Analyzing Industries and Competitors'* Free-Press, originally published 1980.

[58] Porter M.E., *'Competitive Advantage: Creating and Sustaining Superior Performance' Free-Press*, originally published 1985.

[59] Perkins C., *'EU Countries may have known about diesel-emissions manipulation before VW scandal'*, RoadandTrack.com, 19 October 2016.

[60] Campbell P., 'Volkswagen scandal involved 'dozens' of employees - NY lawsuit casts doubt on group's initial defence that only a small number of staff were responsible' *Financial Times* (19 July 2016).

[61] 'Brussels knew carmakers gamed emissions tests before VW scandal' *Financial Times* (17 October 2016).

[62] http://ec.europa.eu/environment/chemicals/reach/reach_en.htm

[63] Christensen C.M., 'Disruptive Technologies: Catching the Wave', *Harvard Business Review* (January-February 1995).

[64] Elgin R. and Ricthe B., *'Fly Me, I'm Freddie: The Biography of Sir Freddie Laker'*, Futura Publications (1981).

[65] Harris M., 'How Branson won the 'dirty tricks' air war', *The Independent* (11 January 1993).

[66] Bothwell C., 'Burberry versus The Chavs', BBC Money Programme / http://news.bbc.co.uk/1/hi/ business/4381140.stm

[67] Krause D.G., 'Sun Tzu The art of War for Executives', Nicolas Brealey Publishing (1995).

[68] Hannas W.C., and Mulvenon J. *'Chinese Industrial Espionage: Technology Acquisition and Military Modernisation'* Routledge, 1st Edition (2013).

[69] Analoui F.,' Workplace sabotage: its styles, motives and management*', Journal of Management Development*, Vol. 14 Issue 7, (2016), p.48 – 65.

[70] DIRECTIVE (EU) 2016/943 of The European Parliament and of The Council, on the protection of undisclosed know-how and business information (trade secrets) against their unlawful acquisition, use and disclosure, June 8, 2016. http://eur-lex.europa.eu/legal-content/EN/TXT/PDF/?uri=CELEX:32016L0943&from=EN

Printed in Great Britain
by Amazon